STINKIN' THINKIN' STINKS

A Kid's guide to the lighter side of life

by:

Bill King

BRYCE CULLEN PUBLISHING

**BRYCE
CULLEN
PUBLISHING**

PO Box 731
Alpine, NJ 07620
brycecullen.com

ISBN 978-1-935752-43-1

Library of Congress Control Number: 2013950190

Printed in the United States of America

10 9 8 7 6 5 4 3 2 1

This book is dedicated to you, the reader, to provide you with the necessary tools to enjoy the "lighter side of life."

TABLE OF CONTENTS

INTRODUCTION

Do you ever find yourself thinking negative thoughts? Maybe you're thinking about how difficult that test tomorrow is going to be and that there is no way you can pass it. Or maybe you're thinking about how much you dislike the kid who sits behind you in class. Maybe you're annoyed with your brother, tired of your mom nagging you about your chores, or annoyed that you have to clean up your room. Or you might be thinking that you will never make the baseball team, don't seem to have any friends, or that you wish you were prettier, a better athlete, or smarter. And you get into a funk. That is STINKIN' THINKIN'.

There are a few things about our thoughts that each of us needs to know:

- The way we think about things often determines the way things are.
- The way we think can become a habit.
- STINKIN' thoughts almost always create STINKIN' results.
- Sweet thoughts, positivity, almost always create positive results.

What does this mean?

Think you can, think you can't; either way, you'll be right. —Henry Ford (American industrialist and pioneer of the assembly-line, 1863–1947)

STINKIN' THINKIN' Translation:

Henry Ford, the founder of what is now Ford Motor Company, said it well when he stated, "Think you can, think you can't; either way, you'll be right." What was he really saying and how does it apply to all of our lives? Henry Ford was telling us that our attitude can determine what we accomplish, what roads we take in life, and how good or bad—how sweet or STINKIN'—our lives will be.

And we also need to know that the way we look at and think about things can become a habit. Whether we make that a good habit or a bad one is up to us.

- How do you generally think?
- What is your attitude usually like?
- Do you invite negativity into your life? Or are you focused on the positive?
- Are you even aware of how you think and how that thinking affects your life?

This book is about assessing *your* thinking and deciding whether you are using it to make your life better or worse. In other words, you are going to figure out if you have developed STINKIN' THINKIN'. If you have, this book will help you change your habits so that your life can be the SA-WEETEST you can make it.

As you read through this book, embrace the funny words. *STINKIN' THINKIN' . . . SA-WEET . . . STINK BUG . . . STENCH.* They are exaggerations meant to make you really think about your thought process, the thoughts of others, and how very powerful thoughts are and what they can lead to.

Do the exercises. You really will learn something important about yourself from every one.

This is going to be informative. This is going to be empowering. And this is going to be fun!

1
WHAT'S ALL THE STINK ABOUT?
UNCOVER NEGATIVITY USING AWARENESS

There is little difference in people, but that little difference makes a big difference. The little difference is attitude. The big difference is whether it is positive or negative. —W. Clement Stone (Author, 1902–2002)

STINKIN' THINKIN' Translation:
People are different because some are positive and
SA-WEET while some are negative and just plain out STINK!

What is your mindset? Before you start reading, take this quiz!

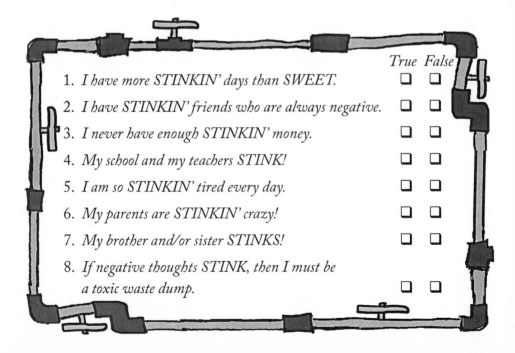

	True	False
1. *I have more STINKIN' days than SWEET.*	☐	☐
2. *I have STINKIN' friends who are always negative.*	☐	☐
3. *I never have enough STINKIN' money.*	☐	☐
4. *My school and my teachers STINK!*	☐	☐
5. *I am so STINKIN' tired every day.*	☐	☐
6. *My parents are STINKIN' crazy!*	☐	☐
7. *My brother and/or sister STINKS!*	☐	☐
8. *If negative thoughts STINK, then I must be a toxic waste dump.*	☐	☐

Do you see life from a negative or a positive point of view? Does your attitude STINK, or is it SWEET? If you answered "true" to two or more of these questions, look out! You probably STINK! Why would you STINK? Because

NEGATIVE THOUGHTS STINK!

Just think about it. When all you think about is how bad everything and everybody are,

YOU FEEL BAD

along with them, don't you? Well, that just STINKS! Some people think about how bad everything and everybody are so much that they forget how to see all the wonderful things around them and how to be happy.

These are STINKIN' people. And the biggest problem with STINK-IN' people and thoughts is that they are contagious. Like big sneezes, they blow their STINKIN' attitude all over everything—and every-one—around them. They have so many negative thoughts all the time, they just SMELL up the place! You know people like this, don't you? They're always talking about how bad things are, and their STINKIN' THINKIN' makes them feel so bad they try to make everyone around them feel terrible too!

But what you will learn by reading this book is that

STINKIN' THINKIN' IS A CHOICE.

Even if you have noticed your negative thinking only recently, or have been thinking negatively for as long as you can remember, or just find yourself susceptible to the negative thinking of others, you can always make a different choice.

You're probably sitting there thinking, "What? I can't *choose* what I think!" But you know what? You can! Try this quick experiment. Pick out your favorite park. It could be one that's down the street or the one at your school.

First, picture the park during a time when someone wasn't being nice to you. They wouldn't take turns, they said something mean to you, they made fun of you, or they excluded you from a game. Got it? Now really focus on that experience. How did you feel when that happened? Notice how your stomach feels as you remember it. What kind of expression is on your face? What else do you notice about the park in your memory? Was there a lot of trash or dirt? Were there a lot of mean kids there? Were parents being mean to their kids?

How do you feel right now? You probably feel pretty bad. That STINKS! Now try the second part of the experiment.

Go back to the same park in your mind. Think about a time when you did something you were really proud of. You jumped out of the swing and landed on your feet, you made the perfect sand castle, or you made friends with another person because you let them go ahead of you in line. You hit a home run in a ball game, won a race, or it was just a bright sunny day and you got to read a great book. Check out your stomach and see how you feel as you remember that good memory. Look around the park in your imagination now. What other things do you notice? Were there smiling people sitting on the benches? Was the sun shining beautifully through the trees? Were there other people being nice that day or doing cool things they were proud of?

Do you feel better after thinking about this second memory than you did after the first? Well, of course you do! Don't you want to feel good more often? Then all you have to do is think about good things more! It's just that easy!

Here's how it works:

WHAT YOU THINK ABOUT EXPANDS.

When we focus on something, it gains importance in our lives. And that importance can take on a positive or a negative tone. For example, if we have a math test coming up, and we want to do well on it, we may plan time to study. Then we may review our work, study, and feel prepared for the test. We tell ourselves that we are going to do great, and we head off to school.

On the other hand, we may be fearful of math and tell ourselves from the git-go that there is no way we will do well on the test. We don't plan to study. If our parents make us study, we are so focused on the fact that we cannot possibly do well that nothing we study sinks in. We go to class expecting to do poorly, and most times that will be exactly what happens. And that sets us up to think about all the other subjects in which we don't expect to do well—and so we don't.

Either way, we thought about that math test, and its importance expanded. But when we let ourselves fall into STINKIN' THINKIN', the expansion was greater—along with the negative effect.

When you let your mind fall into STINKIN' THINKIN', you actually notice a bunch of STINKIN' things in your life. And then you really get in trouble because you think even more negatively. Finally, because you're so STINKY, you actually bring more negative people and things into your life! It becomes a big snowball rolling down a hill, getting bigger and bigger along the way, seeming unstoppable.

But if you choose to think about what's good, guess what? You begin to notice more of the really cool people and stuff in your life. Then, because you are feelin' so SWEET, you truly bring even more cool people and things to you! Is that not just the SWEETEST?

Think about it this way and see if it doesn't make more sense. Picture the ocean. See the birds? See the sailboats? Awesome! This picture in your mind—of all those beautiful things above the water—represents everything that's concrete in the world. It's what you can see, touch, taste, hear, or smell.

Now let your mind travel under the water. See the fish and the seaweed? See the ocean floor? Very cool. This picture in your mind—of all the amazing things *under* the water—represents everything that you can't see, touch, taste, hear, or smell in the world. It's the world of thoughts.

Imagine yourself having a thought that becomes a solid block. The block shoots out of your head and lands in the water. It sinks to the bottom and comes to rest on the ocean floor. Now every time you have a thought like that one, a new block shoots out of your head and lands on top of the first one. Eventually, you have so many similar thoughts that the stack of blocks gets tall enough to break the surface of the ocean! Everything you've been thinking about has become real!

So here's the scoop:

WHEN ALL *YOU* THINK ABOUT IS NEGATIVE, *YOU* FEEL BAD, AND EVERYTHING AROUND *YOU* IS NEGATIVE TOO!

And you can guess what kind of life you will have if you think good thoughts. Yep!

WHEN *YOU* THINK MOSTLY GOOD THOUGHTS, *YOU* FEEL GOOD, AND EVERYTHING AROUND *YOU* BECOMES POSITIVE. *YOU* EXPERIENCE A SA—WEET LIFE!

Nice how that works out, isn't it?

So now you know what all the STINK is about! Negative thoughts STINK. But you can choose what kind of thoughts you think. Your choice will influence what kind of life you have. If you choose thoughts that STINK, your life will STINK, too! But if you remember to focus on all the good things in life, your life will be awesome and you'll feel great!

Of course, there are times when we have negative encounters or when negative events happen. But if we have conditioned or trained ourselves to dwell on positive things, those negative events will be far less likely to take over our lives. In fact, our positive conditioning will help them dissipate—or become less important—and we will be better able to handle them because we are used to focusing on what is good in life.

The time has come to get your STINK out! Reading this book means you don't want to STINK anymore. By reading the following chapters and doing the exercises, you will learn how to train yourself to think more positive thoughts and enjoy a SA-WEET life!

Do each exercise in the following pages with all your heart. Don't skip over them. They're like practicing the piano every day or going to batting practice. At first it might be hard and won't feel natural. But the more you practice, the better you'll be at it. Then one day you'll be ready for Carnegie Hall or Fenway Park. Whoa!

Sweetie
Sweetie changed her thoughts and ultimately changed her life by making positive choices.

And for those of you who are thinking, "I already focus on the positive," good for you! What this will do is reinforce that positive thinking and strengthen your ability to avoid the negative.

YOUR FIRST STINKIN' EXERCISE: WORKING WITH B.L.O.C.K.S.

Your first STINKIN' exercise will help you convert STINKIN' THINKIN' to something much more desirable. This exercise is easy and fun, and since STINKIN' THINKIN' can have devastating results in your life if you don't deal with it, it's just what the doctor ordered. The purpose of the exercise is to start becoming aware of negative thinking and show that you have choices. In every situation, you can let STINK-IN' THINKIN' determine your choice, or you can choose to be kind instead. When you choose kindness, that's a win for everyone!

It's time to play with B.L.O.C.K.S. No, not the ones you played with as a child. Well, not quite. These B.L.O.C.K.S.—short for Building Lively Optimistic Choices Kindly & Successfully—are real, yes, and you can stack them, it's true, but you won't be building walls or towers like you did in preschool. You will be building optimistic choices throughout your day. To complete this exercise, you will need the following items:

- 15 building blocks (The size of the blocks doesn't matter. If you don't have building blocks, make the blocks out of cardboard by cutting out six 2-inch squares and taping them together into a single cube-shaped building block. Do this 15 times.)
- 1 white poster board
- set of markers
- glue
- 3 index cards
- 1 pen or pencil

Getting Your Exercise Ready

Tape the poster board to the floor, on a table, or wherever there is a flat surface. Draw a blue line representing the water of the ocean across the top of the poster board, from left to right, just an inch higher than five building blocks would reach if you stacked them on top of each other to form a line going from the bottom of the poster board upward. Decorate the poster if you like, with sun, stars, fish, clouds, etc.

Your exercise will last three days.

Day 1

Your exercise for today is to become aware of negative thinking and the choices that come with it.

Get the index card and draw a line dividing it in half. Write "Positive Blocks" just above the left side of the line and "Negative Blocks" just above the right side of the line. Each time you have a negative thought, put a mark on the right side. However, each time you are able to change that thought to the positive, put a mark on the Positive Block side.

It works this way. Once you have become aware of a negative thought, notice what follows next in your mind. Because at that point you have a choice: You can choose to have more negative thoughts, or you can change that original thought to something positive.

For example, let's say you have an English test today and on your way to school you think, "Man, I am just no good at English." You have a choice at that moment—you can continue that thinking or you can replace that thought with something positive. To continue that negative thought, you might think, "I am probably going to do badly on my test today." To change it, you could replace the thought with something positive like, "I need to be positive about my chances."

The choice is yours. Which choice will you make? When you get home, make two stacks of building blocks on your poster. One stack will be for the positive marks on the index card—one block for every mark on the positive side of your card—and the other stack will be for the negative marks on the index card—one block for every mark on the negative side of your card.

Stack the building blocks (glue them if they are paper) in a line from the ocean floor upward toward the surface of the water. If you have less than six blocks in either stack, they will not reach the surface yet, but that's okay.

Day 2
Your exercise for today is to repeat the Day 1 exercise.

At the end of the day, stack the building blocks (glue them if they are paper) on top of the lines you started yesterday.

Day 3
Your exercise for today is to see if you can out-stack the negative blocks by changing your thinking to be positive. If you have had two negative days in a row, you will have to work much harder today. But, you can do that, right?

Expected Results
You'll find that when you become aware of negative thinking, you'll realize that you have a choice. You don't have to keep repeating the STINKIN' THINKIN' until you're very sad. The more aware you become of negative thinking, the easier it will be to choose positive thinking instead. The result will be a SA-WEET one, that's for sure. **Positive Thinking Attracts Positive Thinking.**

Tips for a Successful Exercise

- For the first two days, don't judge yourself too harshly if you have a lot of negative thoughts.
- Remember, the exercise is about awareness and choice.
- Go all-out for the exercise. Don't hold anything back.
- If you want to have more positive blocks, each time a nega-

tive thought comes up, decide to do a kind deed for someone. This will keep you from adding to the negative stack because it's very difficult to have negative thinking while doing a kind deed or even thinking of doing a kind deed.

- Be sure to carry your index card and something to write with all day. That way, you won't have to try to remember the marks.

The STINKIN' Summary

- Negative thoughts STINK because they make you feel bad. Since what you think about EXPANDS, you need to be very aware of your thoughts. When you fall into STINKIN' THINKIN', you actually attract more STINKIN' things into your life.
- STINKIN' THINKIN' is a choice. STINKIN' people are simply people who make STINKIN' THINKIN' a habit.
- The B.L.O.C.K.S. exercise illustrates how what you think about EXPANDS. The more you think about negative things, the worse you feel, and more negative things begin to show up in your life. The more SWEET thoughts you have, the better you'll feel, and more and more great things will come into your life.

Choose positive thoughts, and use this book and the exercises in it to practice breaking a STINKIN' THINKIN' habit and to reinforce your SWEET THINKIN'. You'll find that you feel better and better, and you'll notice life being SA-WEETER and SA-WEETER!

2
PLEASE DON'T STINK!
WASH AWAY NEGATIVITY WITH IMAGES

"There are some days I practice positive thinking, and other days I'm not positive I am thinking." —John M. Eades, Ph.D. (Author)

STINKIN' THINKIN' Translation:
If you're STINKIN' THINKIN', stop THINKIN' of STINK!

No one enjoys being around anyone else who STINKS. It's our nature to find SA-WEET people that support us. The COOLEST thing ever is that you don't have to STINK any more with your STINKIN' THINKIN'. Your attitude can go from a STENCH of a raw sewage plant to the SMELL of SWEET roses in no time at all. The earlier you get the STINK out, the better your life will be. It's an absolute guarantee.

You may be asking yourself, "Does this guy ever experience STINKIN' THINKIN'?" And the answer is: sure, every single day.

IT IS VIRTUALLY IMPOSSIBLE TO NOT EXPERIENCE NEGATIVE THINKING.

The fact is we're bombarded every single hour of every single day with STINKIN' things to think about. The key is to choose not to FOCUS on them. When a STINKIN' thought comes up, say to yourself, "Thank you for sharing!" and replace that STINKIN' thought with a positive one. It's actually easier than you think . . . but it requires that you become aware of your STINKIN' THINKIN'.

Things happen that annoy us on a daily basis. We could be riding the school bus or dealing with STINKIN' problems at school. Or maybe we'll have STINKIN' family and friends to deal with. Or maybe we'll be facing some of those STINKIN' things that are out in the world today. It's very difficult not to notice them. It's even harder not to have even more STINKIN' thoughts about them. Just watch the local or national news and you'll discover very quickly how STINKIN' THINKIN' keeps its momentum in our lives. In each of those cases, you are in charge of your own thoughts. You. Decide right here and now that when others try to emit their personal STENCH, you will

SEND SWEET THOUGHTS IN RETURN.

Sending love to everyone in every situation is the best cure for STINK-IN' people with STINKIN' problems.

Is it okay to experience really, really bad STINKIN' thoughts? Sure, and sometimes it can take a while to get the STINKIN' thoughts out of our heads. But you can do it. Really. The difference between SWEET-NESS and STENCH is to not dwell on those STINKIN' thoughts for very long. There are a number of different techniques to get rid of the STINKIN' THINKIN'. One method you can try is to picture yourself as if you were watching a movie starring yourself. See yourself and poke fun at yourself having such a pity party. It might sound something like this: "Look at little Billy. He is so sad. Look, there he goes again, having a pity party for himself. Poor little Billy." After you do this, you can't help but chuckle at yourself. It really does work and usually will change your state of mind almost immediately. Thankfully, once you become aware of your STINKIN' THINKIN', you won't have to do this very often because you'll catch yourself before you have an all-out STINK attack.

Most people will agree that it's always much more beneficial to have a positive attitude. But it takes some work, some conscious effort. Try to see the glass half full instead of half empty at all times. It doesn't matter if your favorite major league baseball team is down five runs with two outs in the bottom of the ninth with no one on and the number nine hitter at the plate. Be positive.

THINK POSITIVE THOUGHTS BECAUSE IT SURE BEATS THE ALTERNATIVE.

What do you have to lose other than a bunch of STINK-IN' THINKIN' wasting your STINKIN' time? Once you start looking at the positive aspect of almost every situation, you will quickly understand the true benefits of positive thinking.

Twiggy
Twiggy loves to imagine taking a mental shower to help her get rid of negative thinking.

No one wants to STINK, period. And no one wants to SMELL the STENCH created by your STINKIN' THINKIN'. One tool you have is visualization. It's very simple and everyone can do it. Sometimes it requires a little more concentration, especially when you're being bombarded with STINKIN' things. Visualization is simply picturing yourself in a positive situation. It is a lot like day dreaming, but its purpose is to get you out of your STINKIN' THINKIN'.

On those days when it seems there's nothing you can do to eliminate the STENCH surrounding you with your STINKIN' THINKIN', it's time to try something completely different. As soon as you start to SMELL yourself on these days, do the exercise below and you'll quickly dissipate the STINK of your negative thoughts. Please, for the love of mankind, don't STINK anymore!

STINKIN' EXERCISE:
CLEAN UP THE STINK

Have you ever had a bad day? Sure, you have. Most of us have struggles from time to time. This exercise was designed to help you on those STINKIN' days. It comes in three parts: a physical shower, a visual shower, and then a comparison. First, you have to become aware of your STINKIN' THINKIN'. When you're having a bad day, you can be sure that there is STINKIN' THINKIN' close by.

This exercise doesn't require much. When you're having a bad day or just experiencing a lot of STINKIN' THINKIN', go directly to your shower and wash up. That's it. Just take a shower, and then journal how you feel immediately after taking your shower.

Here's an example for you. You wake up in the morning and find that something you've been really excited about doing has been canceled. This might be a camping trip or spending the day with friends at a local water park. Then as the day progresses, you find yourself bored with nothing to do. You have now entered the STINK Zone. You start complaining to everyone you know about how miserable your day is. And your complaining suddenly begins to be about your whole life. Once you notice this STINKIN' THINKIN', it's time to hit the showers.

Part 1 of the STINKIN' Exercise

Take a shower and wash really well. Don't take a quick two-minute shower. Make sure it lasts a little longer than normal. Maybe even sing in the shower. When you're done with the shower, pull out a clean piece of paper and write down these two questions:

> Do I feel better?
> What could happen right now to get me excited?

Answer those questions quickly with what comes to your mind first. This is the end of Part 1 of the exercise.

Part 2 of the STINKIN' Exercise

The next time you experience a tough day, take a "Cosmic Shower." This time, no actual water is involved—you'll be taking a shower in your imagination.

Here's what to do: As soon as you recognize that you're having a lousy day, find a quiet place. Sit down in a comfortable position. Turn off all electronic devices. Close your eyes and picture yourself stepping into a shower. When you turn the knob in your imagination, you see that little droplets of light coming out of the showerhead. These light drops are as white as white can be. As they hit your body, picture the light cleansing anything negative you have been experiencing. First, wash your head and picture it clearing out all the STINKIN' THINKIN'. Next, go to your neck, in the throat area. Watch the light droplets clear away negative things you typically say. Then move to your heart. Watch the light droplets bounce off of and then into your heart. Picture cleansing away any unforgiving thoughts you have about other people. Now let the cleansing droplets of light clear any negative thought you have about yourself. Now, turn off the faucet and step out of the shower. Awaiting you is the biggest, whitest, fluffiest, softest towel you've ever seen. It completely wraps around your whole body. Dry off and open your eyes. Take out a clean piece of paper and write down the following questions:

> Do I feel better?
> What could happen right now to get me excited?
> Comments:

Answer those questions quickly, with the first answers that come to mind. This is the end of Part 2 of the exercise.

Part 3: Comparing Your STINKIN' Notes

A day or two later, pull out both sheets of paper with your answers and read them. Compare how you felt immediately after the showers. Write down on a new clean piece of paper the following questions:

> Which shower felt better?
> Which shower had a longer lasting effect?
> Which answer gets your more excited now?

Expected Results

This exercise illustrates the power of visualization. You probably felt better when you took a "cosmic shower." This is because the mind is much more powerful than anything that could be done physically. Also, you will discover that a physical shower will typically make you feel good in the short term but the cosmic shower will make you feel better for a much longer time.

Tips for a Successful Exercise

- This exercise can be done every day if you like. The first time you try it, do so when you are experiencing more than normal negative thinking.

- Have a clean piece of paper and pen ready to use immediately after getting out of either shower.
- Be honest about how you feel. If you took a physical shower and do not feel any better, write that down.
- For best results, take the two showers on different days.

The STINKIN' Summary

- Complete parts 1, 2 and 3 of the exercise on different days.
- Everyone experiences STINKIN' THINKIN' on a daily basis.
- It's really OK to experience STINKIN' THINKIN'; just don't stay there for long.
- Try sending love to each STINKIN' person and situation you deal with.
- Visualization is nothing more than picturing yourself in a future positive situation to help you eliminate STINKIN' THINKIN'.
- Visualization can help when you get a STINK attack.

It's easy to get back in a STINK mode if you're not careful. To avoid this, work on your STINKIN' thoughts daily. Whether you STINK or not is totally up to you. Not sure if you STINK? Read the next chapter to learn about your emotional state and how it's related to directly to your STENCH.

3
THINK YOU STINK?
USE TOOLS TO DETERMINE YOUR STATE

"I'm queen of my own compost heap, and I'm getting used to the smell."
—Ani DiFranco (Singer, Song Writer, and Guitarist, b. 1970)

STINKIN' THINKIN' Translation:
Yea, I STINK. I know it! And that's the choice I'm making.

There's one distinct thing that helps you determine if you STINK: your emotions. When you're not feeling happy or at peace, you can bet there are some STINKIN' thoughts close by. If you let STINKIN' THINKIN' get the best of you, YOU STINK! And, you will continue to STINK until you take action to start SMELLING good again.

LET YOUR EMOTIONS TELL YOU IF YOU'RE STARTING TO SMELL.

You can be sure that if you are anxious, worried, angry, or fearful, negative thinking is present. So use them as a guide to help you start thinking about something positive instead.

A question you might be asking yourself is, "Are you saying that I should never experience negative thinking?" That answer is NO. It's perfectly fine to experience negative thinking. Actually, it's almost impossible not to. You just don't want to stay in that state for too long. Recognize that the negative emotions associated with STINKIN' THINKIN' are giving you a very valuable tool: they let you know something important about yourself.

STINKIN' THINKIN' SERVES A PURPOSE.

STINKIN' THINKIN' is an indicator that lets you know you're not experiencing what you want. Imagine life if you never experienced negative thinking. How could you tell if you needed to take a different action to grow as an individual? How would you know when you needed to change direction? You wouldn't. You'd be stuck making the same decisions over and over again, not learning or growing. The point is to avoid getting stuck in STINKIN' THINKIN'.

A good tool to determine if you STINK is to keep track of your daily STINKIN' thoughts. Carry a pen and paper with you during your day and simply put a mark on the paper each time you become aware of a negative thought. Try it for a few days, back to back. If you have more than ten STINK marks per day, chances are good that you SMELL. You may not STINK really badly, but if you don't do something about it quickly, you're destined to really REEK. Remember, STINKIN' THINKIN' can become a habit, and when it does, the STENCH permeates everything you do.

The world really doesn't want you to STINK anymore, so please, stop STINKIN' everything up with your STINKIN' THINKIN'. Pull out a pen and piece of paper and start tracking those STINKIN' thoughts. Do it now! You deserve to SMELL good, and the people around you will thank you.

Track your STINKIN' thoughts for two weeks. The important thing is to track them every day and not to skip a day. You can do that, right? This causes a minor shift in your unconscious mind, making you more aware of negativity and the need to look for positive thoughts instead. Remember,

EVERYONE HAS STINKIN' DAYS.

Having a STINKIN' day here or there doesn't mean you have to pull out a pen and paper to do this exercise again. But if you have multiple STINKIN' days within a given week, then do go back to this STINK-IN' exercise. It will get you back on track. It's also a good idea to do the exercise every now and then just to make sure you're not starting to STINK without realizing it. After a short time you should be able to catch STINKIN' thoughts immediately after having them and save yourself days of feeling sorry for yourself. Remember, if you're feeling sorry for yourself and having a pity party, you're having a major STINK-IN' THINKIN' episode.

To help you keep your STENCH at a nominal level, there's a tool called a STINK-O-METER that measures your STINKOCITY. The STINK-O-METER can be found on the website www.idontstink.com, and it consists of a quiz that determines if you are becoming a STINK bug.

The quiz offers multiple ways for you to get—and keep!—your STINK out. After you answer seven fun multiple-choice questions, you'll be given a score from 1 to 100, with 1 being the best or SWEETEST, and 100 being the STINKIEST. Does your attitude STINK like SMELLY Garbage, ROTTEN eggs, or TOXIC waste? Or does it SMELL like FRESH-baked bread, roses, or perfume?

The results page provides you with your STINKIN' forecast and your STINKIN' prescription to help you get your STINK out. Is your forecast cloudy with a good chance of STENCH, or is it sunny with SWEET SCENTS all around? The prescription link takes you to ten different exercises you can do. Choose the one that corresponds to your score. Lastly, there's a STINK-O-METER that measures the degree of your STENCH. Enjoy it and share it with your friends.

Silly, you say? Why do all this work to get and stay in a positive place? Because what we think and feel, what we allow ourselves to focus on, creates our reality. In short, how we look at the world and at the people with whom we interact is often what they will become. A negative attitude attracts negative people, events, and energy—just as a positive attitude attracts positive people, events, and energy into our lives.

IT'S EASY TO FALL BACK INTO A STINK MODE IF YOU'RE NOT CAREFUL.

The easiest way to determine if you STINK is to use your emotions as a guide. If you feel anger, hurt, worry, shame, guilt, hate, or any kind of fear, and if you allow yourself to dwell on those feelings, you are STINKIN' for sure. The best method to get and keep your STINK out is to work on your STINKIN' THINKIN' every day for at least two weeks. Vow to track those STINKIN' thoughts every day, no matter how many or how few. In as little as two weeks, you can get yourself back on a positive track, seeing and celebrating all the positive things life has to offer. You may still have STINKIN' thoughts regularly, but becoming aware of them will help you turn them around. With your newfound awareness of STINKIN' THINKIN', you'll discover that you can change how you react in the future. Instead of getting into a severe negative state such as worry or blame, you'll be able to recognize the STINKIN' THINKIN' and choose a better response. Even better, you may be able to eliminate the negative state altogether.

For most people, it takes a while before significant overall change in STINKIN' THINKIN' occurs. So, don't be discouraged if you don't have immediate success. However, if you do the exercise for the entire two weeks, you'll see a major improvement when comparing the first and the fourteenth day of the tracking.

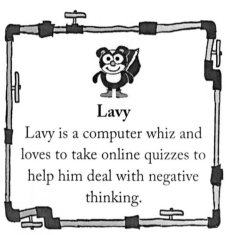

Lavy

Lavy is a computer whiz and loves to take online quizzes to help him deal with negative thinking.

STINKIN' EXERCISE:
DO I STINK?

This exercise was designed to help you determine if you STINK. It provides an opportunity to see how bad your STINKIN' THINKIN' is and offers a prescription for getting your STINK out for good.

This exercise requires only a few minutes to complete. All you need are the following items:

- a computer
- an internet connection
- a pen or pencil and a piece of paper

If you don't have computer access at home, you can use a computer at most libraries—for FREE! Your school library probably even has one.

STEP 1: Type this in your address bar: www.idontstink.com.

STEP 2: Click on the barrel that says "Think You Stink?"

STEP 3: Click "Start."

STEP 4: Fill in your first name.

STEP 5: Answer the 7 questions. Don't be a stinker... ANSWER HONESTLY!

STEP 6: Write down your score.

STEP 7: Read "Your STINKIN' Forecast" to see what the future has in store for you!

STEP 8: Click on "Your STINKIN' Prescription" and follow the prescription guidelines.

Take the STINKIN' quiz for seven straight days, at least once a day. Each time you take the quiz, don't forget to write down your score. Is this number going up or going down? Remember, you want the score to be LOW! 100 is the STINKIEST you can get, so aim for a low score!

Expected Results
While the STINKIN' quiz may be funny at first, each question has a very important meaning. When you answer honestly, you'll get a score to determine if you STINK or if you SMELL great. You may be surprised to see that it takes only a few negative thoughts to spoil the way you SMELL.

If you're honest when you answer the questions, you'll more than likely get a less appealing score than you'd like. This is OK. The goal of this quiz is to bring awareness to your negative thinking and to allow you to start changing STINKIN' THINKIN' to the SWEET perfume of positivity.

Tips for a Successful Exercise

- If you don't see an answer that you feel is appropriate for you, choose the answer that's closest to how you feel.
- Check out your STINKIN' Forecast to determine what's in store for your near future.
- Try some of the STINKIN' Prescriptions to help you become aware of STINKIN' THINKIN'.
- Write down your score as soon as you see it come up. When you click on other sections such as the Forecast or Prescription, you can't go back to the page that has the score posted; you'd have to take the quiz over.
- Take the quiz periodically to see how you're progressing.
- Enjoy the quiz. Just for fun, try selecting the most negative answers and see what comes up.
- Play with friends by taking turns. See how many different answers you can get.

The STINKIN' Summary

- Your emotional state is directly related to your level of STENCH.
- Always use your emotions as your indicator to determine if you STINK.
- STINKIN' THINKIN' serves a purpose.
- Realize that when you are feeling down, depressed, angry or any other negative emotion, and you wallow in it, you STINK!

- When you are feeling good about yourself: feeling love, happiness, or any other positive emotion, you are one SWEET smelling puppy!
- To keep your STENCH at a tolerable level, try tracking your STINKIN' thoughts on a daily bases for at least two weeks.
- Pay very close attention to any negative state you might be in. As you struggle, imagine that you're oozing out STINKY SMELLS. Remember, it's really okay to experience negative thinking, just don't stay in that state for a long time.

Think you STINK? Go to www.idontstink.com and take the online quiz. The STINK-O-METER will determine your level of STINK-OCITY. Don't worry if you STINK; there's a Forecast section as well as a Prescription link to help you wash away your STENCH.

4

AVOID BECOMING STINK BAIT
FRIENDSHIP POOLS THAT NEED CHLORINE

"BAIT, n. A preparation that renders the hook more palatable."
—Ambrose Bierce (Writer, Journalist, and Editor, 1842–1914)

STINKIN' THINKIN' Translation:
You really don't want to be attracted to STINK bait
because you'll attract a bunch of STINKIN' people!

Negative thoughts STINK. You really don't want other people's STINK to rub off on you. And you certainly don't want to become STINK bait yourself, attracting more STINKIN' thoughts and STINKIN' people!

What is STINK bait? It's something you use when fishing for catfish; that's what it is. And that's not good, because catfish are among the DIRTIEST fish around. They're bottom feeders that prey on STINKIN' things, which is why STINK bait works so well. Much like a magnet to metal, these fish are naturally attracted to anything SMELLY. So here's a question: Are your STINKIN' thoughts attracting some STINKIN' people to your life?

No one likes being around STINK bait! STINK bait is anything SMELLY that attracts other gross things to it. For example, what do you typically see flying around your SMELLY trashcan outside? Flies, of course, because they are attracted to SMELLY things, just like STINK-IN' people are attracted to other STINKIN' people.

SOME PEOPLE ARE ATTRACTED TO PEOPLE THAT SMELL GOOD, WHILE OTHERS ARE ATTRACTED TO PEOPLE THAT SMELL BAD.

The bottom line is that your STINKIN' THINKIN' attracts other people who have STINKIN' THINKIN', and that's not a good combination. If you want a happy and productive life, don't become STINK bait and attract other STINKIN' people into your life.

The more you indulge in STINKIN' THINKIN', the more STINKIN' thoughts and STINKIN' people you will attract. It's like one STINKIN' thought attracts at least three more STINKIN' thoughts, and you start to attract other STINKIN' people who have STINKIN' thoughts themselves. And then, those STINKIN' thoughts attract more STINKIN' thoughts and more STINKIN' people with STINKIN' thoughts. In other words in a very short time, YOU STINK! They STINK! And next thing you know, the health department has quarantined your entire neighborhood due to the hazardous waste you're creating around yourself.

A good test to see if you are becoming STINK bait is to take a good look around you.

LIKE ATTRACTS LIKE.

Are your friends people you look up to or down upon? What kinds of things do they say about other people? What kinds of things do they say about themselves? How do they respond when others say STINKIN' things? Do they join in or try to turn the situation toward the positive? Do they complain a lot? The answers to these questions are clues to your own STINKOCITY. Remember that you are responsible for the friends you choose. If you have STINKIN' friends, chances are good that you have a little STENCH yourself.

Please don't STINK anymore! The world wants you to SMELL good. How can you avoid becoming STINK bait and start to SMELL really good?

TO AVOID BECOMING STINK BAIT, THE KEY IS AWARENESS.

The problem with most people is that they don't realize that they're victims of STINKIN' THINKIN' and as a result don't do anything about it. Don't worry if you SMELL just a little because you had a few STINKIN' thoughts. That's perfectly acceptable. And if you're aware of your STINKIN'

Stanky
Stanky is STINK bait for others because he ignores his negative thinking.

thoughts early enough, you can prevent yourself from becoming a full-out STINKIN' person. Now, how SWEET is that?

Do everything within your power to eliminate STINKIN' THINKIN'. Start becoming aware of your STINKIN' thoughts because awareness will change your whole STINKIN' life. Awareness is equal to SMELL-ING good. STINK bait is equal to SMELLING bad. Which choice are you going to make?

STINKIN' EXERCISE:
STINK BAIT BUDDIES

It's really helpful to know if you *are* STINK bait or *in the process of becoming* STINK bait, and this exercise will help you determine if you are either. You'll be given the opportunity to evaluate your friends and your way of thinking as it relates to the past and the present.

You'll need the following items for this STINKIN' exercise:

- 1 piece of paper
- a pen or pencil

To start this STINKIN' exercise, get out a sheet of paper. Write the statements listed below in the example, then add two columns to the right labeled "Past" and "Present." Next, answer either "Yes" or "No" for each statement in each column. The idea with this exercise is to help you identify if you were STINK bait in the past and determine if you are currently STINK bait.

Example:	Past	Present
1. My best friend supports me.	Yes	No
2. I have really good friends.	Yes	Yes
3. My friends help me when I struggle at school or with my family.	Yes	No
4. My friends listen to me when I need a shoulder.	Yes	Yes
5. My friends never talk badly about others.	Yes	No
6. This is an awesome year for me.	Yes	No
7. I draw appropriate boundaries with my friends.	No	No
8. I rarely have negative thinking.	No	No
9. I never gossip about others.	Yes	No
10. I seldom get angry with my friends.	No	No
	7	2

Now, add up the "Yes" answers from the column titled Past. Then do the same for the Present column. For each "Yes" answer, give yourself one point. For each "No" answer, you will get zero points. In the example above, the score for the Past is 7 while the score for the Present is 2. The idea with this exercise is to identify a trend. If you score below seven in the Past column, you just might have been STINK bait. If you score below seven in the Present column, you are at risk of becoming STINK bait now. This exercise can be repeated three to four times a year; however, for best results, redo this exercise monthly. The constant repetition can help you identify if you are becoming STINK bait before you actually *are* STINK BAIT, and then you can do something about it before it's too late.

Expected Results

While this exercise may only take a few minutes to complete, the results will show you whether or not you're attracting STINKIN' things and STINKIN' people to your life, whether you are going in a positive or a negative direction. Typically, when you're becoming STINK Bait, negative events will follow. Once you identify you are becoming STINK bait, it's up to you to change and get yourself on a more positive track.

Tips for a Successful Exercise

- Plan on spending some time evaluating the statements before you answer.
- Don't rush through it. Really think through each answer.
- When answering, try to be consistent and honest with yourself.
- Repeat the exercise monthly even if the Past answers do not change.
- For the Past column, use 12 months ago or longer when answering the statements.
- For the Present, use the last three months up to today's date.

The STINKIN' Summary

- STINK bait is defined as anything that's SMELLY and attracts SMELLY things to it.
- Some people are attracted to things that STINK, while others are attracted to things that smell SWEET.
- Typically, each negative thought attracts at least three additional negative thoughts.
- Awareness is the key to determining if you are STINK bait.
- Ask yourself questions about your friends and the people with whom you surround yourself to determine if you're becoming STINK bait.

Just remember, if you're emitting the fragrance of DIRTY TOILET WATER, other STINKIN' people that like that SMELL will be attracted to you. UHHHGGGG! Then, as you attract these other STINKIN' people, you also get the bonus of being around their STINKIN' friends. Man, that's a whole a lot of STINK!

5
HOW TO AVOID
CATCHING THE STINK EYE
BE CAREFUL OF WHAT YOU SEE

"As a man is, so he sees. As the eye is formed, such are its powers."
—William Blake (Mystic, Poet, Painter, and Engraver, 1757–1827)

STINKIN' THINKIN' Translation:
If you look for the STINK in things, you'll see a bunch of
STINKIN' things. And if you look for the SA-WEET
in things, you'll see a bunch of SWEET things.

Have you ever heard the phrase "STINK eye?" The dictionary definition of "STINK eye" is as follows: a facial expression of distrust, disdain, or disapproval; also called "hairy eyeball." Do you see things from a STINK eye's point of view?

Here's a slightly different meaning to consider. In this chapter, when you see "STINK eyes," it will refer to how you see something and, without thinking, turn it into something negative. This means that you can see something perfectly harmless, but with your STINK eye you give it a negative meaning. For example, you walk outside and you see two of your best friends walking past your house. Your STINK eye makes you squint just a little and puts your emotions on alert, creating a very negative attitude as they walk past. You immediately think they are trying to leave you out. You instantly feel angry, sad, and lonely. The crazy thing about this is that you do this in less than a few seconds, without even being aware of it. You could find out later that they are planning a surprise birthday party for you and trying to keep it a secret. All that STINKIN' THINKIN' was just a waste of time and energy. Wow! That's a whole lot of useless STINK in a very short time!

If you want to have a positive outlook on life,

YOU HAVE TO GET THE STINK EYE OUT.

One way to get it out is to use some "STINKIN' eye drops." You can't buy them in a store, and they don't come in a liquid form. These drops help you become aware that you're developing a STINK eye, and then they wash the STINK eye away so you can see clearly.

Too many people tend to look for the bad in everything before the good. Some even do this consciously and on purpose. They want to see things from the worst possible point of view so that they can be prepared just in case it comes true. Well, if you use that strategy, more than likely you will actually experience that worst case scenario much more often than someone who gets their STINK eye out!

Dr. Wayne Dyer uses a very effective saying that will help you with a STINK eye. He says,

"IF YOU CHANGE THE WAY YOU LOOK AT THINGS, THE THINGS YOU LOOK AT CHANGE."

That might sound like a play on words, but what it really does is provide a quick solution to STINK eye. When you start becoming aware of your STINK eye, you'll stop looking for the bad and start looking for the beauty and good in all things. And you'll find that having a more positive outlook on life gives you a lot more energy.

Look at a mirror on the side of a car. Do you see the words "objects are closer than they appear"? While that may seem like a dirty trick at first, those words make you aware that what you see in the mirror isn't necessarily accurate; you need to turn your head and look around the car for yourself.

Skids

Skids has a bad case of the STINK eye because he only looks for the bad in everything he sees.

You could say the same about STINK eyes because, if you aren't aware of how they can distort things, you may not stop to consider what's *really* around you. What your STINK eye tells you is bad may actually be harmless or even good. When you get your STINK eye out, you'll start to see the good in almost everything you experience. There's an old saying about making lemonade from lemons. Think of the negative things that happen as lemons, as something that can sour your life. It's up to you to decide whether you want to focus on the sour or take advantage of the lemons, add a little sugar and water, and make lemonade! It's the same with negative events. For example, when you see an accident, do you notice just the horror of the accident, or do you notice how many people are helping the victims and the compassion they are showing? The point of view you assume in every situation you face is up to you.

STINK EYES ARE VERY, VERY CONTAGIOUS.

They spread like wildfire if they aren't contained. For your safety and for everyone around you, there's a STINKIN' COOL exercise to help you avoid catching the STINK eye from anyone else. Consider it a vaccination for your sight. The solution is called the "Cool Shades For STINK Eyes." This exercise can help you see the positive in all situations. Here's to your STINK-Free sight.

STINKIN' EXERCISE:
COOL SHADES FOR STINK EYES

Cool shades for STINK eyes will help you see more clearly throughout your day. They will build your awareness about how you look at things, while developing skills to help you manage a bad case of the STINK eye.

To start your cool shades exercise, you will need the following products:

- seven 3 x 5 index cards (or pieces of paper cut to 3 x 5 size)
- a pencil or pen
- a pair of sunglasses
- seven straight days to do the short exercise (15 minutes each day)

Now, let's get started. The exercises below are short but will take seven days. You can do that, right?

Day 1: Get one index card and a pen or pencil and start looking around. Your job is to notice all the things that you <u>do not</u> like for 15 minutes. Don't apply any judgment to what you notice, just become aware of the things you don't like or that cause you to feel bad. Each time you see something that you don't like or that makes you feel bad or sad, write it down using just one word. For example, if you see a dirty room, write "room." If you see someone you don't like, write his or her first name. If you see a mean dog, write "dog." Use the front and back of the card if you need the space.

Ideas for how and when to do your exercise:

- walk around your house
- go for a walk
- ride in a car
- go to a sporting event
- on your way to school
- between recesses
- on your way home

Day 2: Repeat Day 1 exercise using a new card.

Day 3: Get one index card and a pen or pencil. Put your cool shades on and start looking around. This time, notice all the things that you *like*, that make you feel good, or that put a smile on your face. Do this for 15 minutes. For example, if you see a nice, clean cut backyard, write "yard." If you see a friend, write your friend's first name. If you see your new game system, write the system's name. Continue to write things you see that provoke positive thoughts during the short 15-minute exercise.

Day 4: Repeat Day 3 exercise using a new card.

Day 5: Repeat Day 3 exercise again using a new card.

Day 6: Get the sixth index card and write "Like" on one side and "Don't Like" on the other. Your job today is to write down the things you notice that you like on the "Like" side of the card, and write the things you see that aren't pleasing to you on the "Don't Like" side of the card. Today, don't put on your cool shades. Try this exercise for thirty minutes.

Day 7: Repeat Day 6 exercise, but this time put on the cool shades for the entire exercise.

Expected Results

By Day 7, you'll probably write more things on the "Like" side of the index card than on the "Don't Like" side. That's great! From now on, when you use the cool shades, you'll find yourself looking for things you like more quicklyand you will find more things that you like. This is due to the programming of your mind during the third through fifth days. Cool shades are amazing, aren't they?

Tips for a Successful Exercise

- Go to different places each day.
- Keep an upbeat attitude.
- Don't judge what you don't like, just notice it and write it down.
- Expect that you will see more positive things than negative.
- Focus on the good for days three through seven.

The STINKIN' Summary

- STINK eyes distort what you see and inject negativity.
- Become aware of how you look at things.
- STINK eyes are very contagious.
- Having a STINK eye is a choice.
- Cools shades will help you see what you like.

STINK eyes typically take perfectly harmless situations and make them appear negative. Everything appears worse than it really is. Avoid catching the STINK eye at all costs.

6
HOW TO
ELIMINATE STINK BREATH
BECOME AWARE OF WHAT YOU SAY

"The clever cat eats cheese and breathes down rat holes with baited breath."
—W. C. Fields (Comic and Actor, 1880–1946)

STINKIN' THINKIN' Translation:
You're not a cat so don't try to snare a bunch of STINKY
rodents with your FOUL STENCH because it might just work!

Y'know, mama was right. If you don't have anything good to say about someone, don't say anything at all. It's amazing how true that statement really is. You see, when you open your STINKIN' mouth and let out a bunch of STINKIN' things, you're doing no one any good, including yourself. When you blast everyone with STINKIN' THINKIN', you actually have something called "STINK breath." It's a common side effect of STINKIN' THINKIN', and most people who have it aren't aware that other people can SMELL it. If you use negative words on a regular basis, you're certain to have some form of STINK breath.

So, how can you know if you have STINK breath when you're not aware of the words you use? That's the easy part. You just have to practice being aware of what you say. It really is easier than you think, and the STINKIN' exercise in this chapter will help you change what you say.

Don't take this exercise lightly, because STINK breath is serious. Some people are even STINK-breathoholics! They say STINKIN' things all of the time, and even go out of their way to say negative things about other people. That is a serious case of STINK breath!

STINK BREATH IS ONE OF THE MOST CONTAGIOUS FORMS OF STINKIN' THINKIN' KNOWN TO EXIST.

As soon as someone starts talking negatively about something in his or her life, others typically join in. In a very short time, everyone in the room is telling everyone else all their problems and frustrations. While it's completely okay to discuss your problems, you need to do it in a "controlled" manner, one that focuses on finding solutions instead of wallowing in the negative. Wallowing, or focusing on the negative, causes STINK breath. And when everyone joins in, the STENCH in the room from STINK breath creates the biggest FUNK of all! And it's highly contagious, with those who catch it quickly spreading it to others. Not good at all!

STINK BREATH TYPICALLY
DWELLS ON THE PAST.

Most of the time, when people are made aware of the negative things they've said, they wish they'd kept their mouth shut. That may happen to you when you do this exercise. But the past is done, and there's nothing you can do to change it. If you made mistakes, accept them, ask for forgiveness if necessary, and then move on. The key is to learn from your experience so that you don't repeat the same mistake. This includes both talking negatively about others and relentlessly focusing on negative situations.

When you're with a group of friends or acquaintances, it's not difficult to "sniff" out the ones who have STINK breath. Just notice what they're saying and how they're saying it. Then you can choose either not to add anything or to add something positive about what they're talking about. Just be sure not to add your own negative comments, or you too will suffer from STINK breath. Remember, STINK breath is the most highly contagious form of STINKIN' THINKIN' on the planet.

STINK breath packs a big wallop. Even if you have it for just a very short time, the impact of that STINK breath episode can last a very long time. Think about that for a moment. If you say something hurtful to or about a friend or a family member, it can take a long time to be forgiven. In some cases, you might not ever be forgiven. You do not want to go there. This doesn't mean that you need to say only positive things one hundred percent of the time. That is entirely impossible, anyway. It means that

IF YOU HAVE TO SAY SOMETHING THAT
WOULD SEEM NEGATIVE TO SOMEONE,
DO SO PRIVATELY AND WITH COMPASSION.

For example, if someone you know is behaving inappropriately, realize that they may not be aware of it. Don't make fun of them. Don't embarrass them by correcting them in front of others. Instead, gently let them know their behavior is inappropriate and why, without others hearing, or even change the subject entirely. Often, that's all it takes to make someone aware of their inappropriate behavior.

ONE OF THE KEY STEPS TO ELIMINATING STINK BREATH IS TO BECOME AWARE OF WHAT YOU SAY.

Get into the habit of noticing what you're saying, and with practice you can catch yourself before you say something that STINKS. For example, listen very carefully to what follows immediately after the words "I am…" The words "I am" are the most powerful affirmations you can say about yourself, and the words that follow it have deep meaning.

An affirmation is a statement that confirms either a prior judgment or a previous decision about yourself, whether it is true or not. Notice that I used the words "judgment" and "decision."

Did you know you could affirm something that is completely untrue? The definition of a STINKY affirmation is affirming something about yourself or a situation that is completely false. You can say, "I am a complete idiot!" OUCH! Do people really do that? Of course they do, but that doesn't make it true!

There is great power in affirmations. Isn't it interesting that people tend to experience exactly what they affirmed? To illustrate this, here's a very powerful example for you to see the power of STINK breath and STINKY affirmations.

When I was in middle school, I recall my mom saying, "You just don't read very fast." Somehow I adopted that frame of mind and used it as an excuse if I didn't do well on reading tests and quizzes. I affirmed my belief on a regular basis saying, "I am a slow reader." And for 35 years I experienced slow reading—and only read when I had to.

I would always score poorly on standardized tests because I kept affirming that I was a slow reader. I can recall taking the college entrance exam and checking to see how much I had to read in each section. If it was too long, I told myself that I could not finish it and in every instance, I didn't. Suffice it to say I didn't score very high!

When I was in my mid-thirties, I started reading books for fun. Instantly, my mind told me, "I'm a slow reader." At that moment, I realized that I had a choice. I decided to change my old belief that I was a slow reader to something more positive. I started to affirm, "I am a fast reader and I comprehend everything that I read."

Rotten

Rotten suffers from STINK breath because he always says negative things about himself and others.

From that moment onward, I read books at lightning speed compared to my old way. Now I regularly read five to six books at a time, and I can read huge novels in only a week or two. Previously, it would take me so long to read a long book that I would just give up—or not try at all. When I changed my affirmation about myself, a whole new world opened up to me.

Do you say any negative affirmations about yourself? Do you use negative words to describe even the things you like? Not to worry, just brush your breath with this STINKIN' COOL exercise.

STINKIN' EXERCISE: BRUSH YOUR BREATH WITH STINK—EASE MINTS

Because STINK breath is so contagious, it's important to keep your breath fresh and clean of STINKY words. The solution to STINK breath is finally here in the form of a breath mint. STINK-EASE Mints neutralize the ODOR created by STINK breath. They work perfectly every time, and you can use them as often as necessary.

For this exercise you will need the following:

- 2 small containers of breath mints, such as Tic Tacs
- a marker
- a 3" x 5" index card
- a pen or pencil

This exercise will take place over a three-day period. To start the exercise, you will empty one of the breath mint containers. (Put them in a clean, dry container for another time.) Start your day with one full and one empty container.

To prevent confusing the containers during the exercise, use the marker to write a big "F" on the full container and a big "E" on the empty one. Then, if you have pockets, put the full pack of mints in your left pocket and the empty pack in your right one. If you are carrying a backpack, you can put them in different pockets.

Day 1
Your exercise is to notice the negative words people use. Each time you hear something negative, grab the full pack of mints, take one mint out and put it in the empty one. Continue this all day.

At night, count the number of mints that have been placed in the empty pack. Pull out your index card and write down "Day 1 - _____" and enter the number of mints you moved into the blank.

Day 2
Start the day just as you did on Day 1, with the full and the empty containers. Today, you will notice the negative words *you* choose throughout your day. Each time you hear yourself say anything negative, take one mint out of the full pack and place it into the empty pack.

At night, count the number of mints that have been placed in the empty pack. Pull out your index card and write down "Day 2 - _____" and enter the number of mints you moved into the blank. Add the two days' count and write "Total - _____" and enter the total number of negative statements for both days.

Day 3
Start your day by emptying out both packs of mints. Leave one empty and set it aside. Then fill the other one with the same number of mints from the total of the two days.

For example:
> Day 1 – 10 mints
> Day 2 – 5 mints
> Total – 15 mints
>
> Day 3 – Pack 1 – put in 15 mints
> Pack 2 – leave empty

Your exercise on day 3 is to use positive words when speaking with other people. This exercise cannot be done alone. You must be in conversation with others. It can be in person or it can even be over the phone, but you must say the positive things out loud. Each time you say something positive, take one of the mints out of the pack containing the mints and place it into the empty one. The goal for the day is to say enough positive things that you empty out the full pack of mints and move them all to the empty one.

Expected Results

This exercise might be a little difficult at first, but don't worry. It's designed to help you become aware of not only what you say, but also what others are saying. The first time you do this exercise, don't be alarmed if you can't empty the pack of mints on the third day. You may have to repeat the exercise several times before you accomplish that goal.

Tips for a Successful Exercise

- Don't try this on any days when you are mostly alone.
- Try to use the positive words you choose in such a way that others don't know what you're doing. For example, don't use multiple positive words in a row because that would be too obvious—and would only count for one mint.
- Try the exercise on one friend or family member.
- If you're in a group of people and it would be very obvious to keep pulling out the packs of mints, simply keep a mental count and switch the mints at a later time.
- If you run out of mints on either of the first two days, start switching the mints back to the original pack and take note.
- Suggestions of positive words you can use on Day 3:
  - Super
  - Fabulous
  - Happy
  - Joyful
  - That Rocks!
  - Thank you.
  - Love
  - Delicious
  - Fantastic
  - I can do it!

- o Great!
- o Kind
- o Positive
- Pick a friend and try doing the exercise together. Then compare your results each day.

The STINKIN' Summary

- STINK breath is the negative words that you use on a daily basis.
- Most people don't know that they have STINK breath.
- Most STINK breath episodes focus on past events.
- STINK breath is a highly-contagious form of STINKIN' THINKIN'.
- Compassion helps with STINK breath.
- Affirmations can be positive or negative. They are very powerful. Try to make them positive, whether they are about yourself or someone else. When saying "I am ____" or "You are ___.", fill in the blanks with only positive words.
- Use STINK-EASE mints daily to maintain a positive vocabulary.

STINK breath is debilitating. It occurs when you use negative words on a regular basis. Most people don't know that they have STINK breath because they're not aware of the words they use and don't think about the impact they have on themselves or others.

One way to eliminate STINK breath is to use powerful affirmations. The most powerful affirmation that you can use begins with the words "I am." Be very, very careful with what you say after those two words.

When you need to have a talk with someone who seems negative, do so privately and with compassion. A good way to do this is to start the conversation with "Because I love you..." or "Because I care about you..."

and then have your discussion.

You will start to experience a different kind of day when you make positive words your new daily standard.

7

TAKE OUT
YOUR STINKIN' TRASH
TRACK NEGATIVE THINKING

"I know a man who doesn't pay to have his trash taken out. How does he get rid of his trash? He gift wraps it, and puts it into an unlocked car."
—Henry Youngman (British-born comedian and violinist, 1906–1998)

STINKIN' THINKIN' Translation:
If you take out your trash daily, you won't
have to SMELL it in other people's cars.

What do you do when something in your house SMELLS? You put it in the trash and immediately take it outside to your trash bin or dumpster, of course! You don't even have to think about it. The moment you SMELL it, you trash it. That's exactly what you should do with all your STINKIN' THINKIN'.

GET THOSE STINKIN' THOUGHTS OUT OF YOUR HEAD—IMMEDIATELY!

The moment you become aware of negative thoughts, or for that matter SMELL them, trash them.

There's really not a lot to talk about in this chapter. With trash, you identify the STINKIN' source and get rid of what SMELLS. The same holds true for STINKIN' THINKIN'. Since we've already established that negative thoughts STINK, once you start to SMELL your negative thinking, you have to use tools to help you get rid of them.

We've learned that most people aren't aware of STINKIN' THINKIN'. Heck, most people don't even think about their thoughts at all. And when you're not aware of negative thinking, you continue to allow it to control your emotional state most of the time. Not a good plan at all.

THE VERY FIRST STEP TOWARDS GETTING RID OF STINKIN' THINKIN' IS TO BECOME AWARE OF YOUR PREDOMINANT THOUGHTS.

Bruiser
Bruiser is very shy and rarely takes out his STINKIN' trash because he ignores his negative thoughts.

Only when you become aware of negative thinking can you start to make different choices that will support your highest good. The more aware you are of your STINKIN' THINKIN', the less STINKIN' THINKIN' you'll have. Now that is a SA-WEET tradeoff!

If you're ready to get your STINK out, try the following STINKIN' exercise and you'll be well on your way to not STINKIN' anymore. In fact, you'll begin to SMELL GOOD! And when you SMELL GOOD, you're able to change the STENCH of your immediate surroundings. So go on, SMELL GOOD and share that GOOD SMELL with others in your house, your neighborhood, your school, your work, and your entire town.

STINKIN' EXERCISE:
TAKE OUT YOUR STINKIN' TRASH

This exercise was designed to help you become aware of STINKIN' THINKIN' and take action to eliminate it. You can't do anything about it if you don't even know you have it. The more you work this exercise, the more you'll become aware of just how much STINKIN' THINKIN' you do. This is an exercise that will have you reaping benefits for the rest of your life! When you discover your STINKIN' THINKIN', remember to not judge yourself too harshly. We all have negative thoughts. It's impossible to not have them. Use this exercise to become aware of them and work on changing them, and then watch SWEET success after success come your way.

Before starting, you will need the following items:

- 1 small notepad

- a pen or pencil
- 7 full sheets of blank paper

To start, get the small notepad and carry it with you all day. It doesn't matter where you go or what you do, carry it with you. Do this every day for the next week. **Every time a STINKIN' thought pops up, say, "Thank you for sharing. I'm becoming aware of my STINKIN' THINKIN'."** Then take the pencil or pen and put a mark in the notepad. Just before going to bed, add all the marks up. Once you know your total, your task is to write something positive on one of the full sheets of blank paper for every mark on your list. Before you start writing your positive statements, say the following: "I am taking out my STINKIN' Trash!"

Here's an example: On the first day, you have 25 marks on your pad. Say the following: "I am taking out my STINKIN' Trash!" Next, write 25 positive statements. They can be about yourself, your friends, family, events, goals, school, or anything that is positive. 1) My mom and dad are so nice to me. 2) I am such a kind person. 3) I love my house. 4) My friends are so cool. 5) I have such a good time playing with my pet. Continue until you get to 25.

The next morning, pull out your list and read each positive statement before getting out of bed. During the second day, continue to track negative thoughts just like the day before. Repeat the nightly exercise by writing positive statements for the same number of marks. Continue this exercise for seven days in a row.

Expected Results

The purpose of this exercise is to make yourself more aware of your STINKIN' thoughts and to start to change them on a daily basis. As you become more aware of them, you'll naturally start to see the daily number drop. Sometimes you'll even catch yourself before you have the next STINKIN' thought. You'll notice that you're saying kinder things because you don't want to make any more STINKIN' marks for that day.

Tips for a Successful Exercise

- Be sure to carry a pen/pencil and a small notepad with you all day.
- Stick with the exercise for all seven days.
- Write a mark every time you have a thought that has any kind of negative meaning to you.
- Make sure that you wake up a few minutes early in the morning.
- If you don't have time to read your list before you get out of bed, you can read them on the bus, in the car on the way to school, or anytime in the morning. For best results, read them before you start tracking your negative thoughts for that day.
- Keep the results stored away so you can compare the numbers the next time you do the exercise.

The STINKIN' Summary

- The first step in identifying STINKIN' THINKIN' is to become aware of it.
- "Take Out Your STINKIN' Trash" is a very powerful exercise for clearing your mind of STINKIN' thoughts and eliminating future negative thoughts.
- Don't be alarmed if you have a lot of STINKIN' THINKIN'. This exercise is about awareness. It is about learning. Don't judge yourself harshly.

This exercise puts you in control of the way you think. By completing this exercise, you have taken the STINKIN' thoughts out of your head and put them in the trash where they belong. Try it for seven days and SMELL the difference for yourself.

8
HOW TO
DIFFUSE A STINK BOMB
ELIMINATE GOSSIP WITHIN YOUR GROUP

"Gossip is a sort of smoke that comes from the dirty tobacco-pipes of those who diffuse it: it proves nothing but the bad taste of the smoker."
—George Eliot (English Victorian Novelist 1819–1880)

STINKIN' THINKIN' Translation:
Keep your STINKIN' mouth shut if you
don't have something SWEET to say.

What in the world is a "STINK bomb," and how could it relate to STINKIN' THINKIN'? A STINK bomb is like a firecracker without the bang. Its bang is its STINKIN' SMELL. After you light the fuse, clouds of smoke erupt from it, giving anyone around it a really bad STINK! STINK bombs are used for simple pranks, and there are even military-grade concoctions available. The STINKIN' THINKIN' STINK bombs in this chapter relate to gossip. Yep, gossip. And we all know how ugly that can get.

These STINK bombs are very similar to the STINK bombs you may already know about. But instead of making people run away from them, they actually attract STINKIN' THINKIN' people to them. And man, when a STINK bomb goes off and a lot of STINKIN' people come together, a massive STINKIN' explosion is sure to follow.

STINK BOMBS CAN BE CONTROLLED.

STINK bombs can be diffused, if you know enough about what causes them. It takes a little practice, but you can do it. The exercise at the end of this chapter will guide you through diffusing a STINK bomb with calculated precision. Just remember, if you are not careful, you could set off your own STINK bomb and create a chain reaction of other STINK bombs.

STINK BOMBS REQUIRE MORE THAN ONE PERSON TO IGNITE.

The way they typically operate is one person lights the fuse (makes the negative statement about another person) and then at least one more person delivers the STINK bomb (adds their own negative statement). In larger groups the shock effects of a STINK bomb can be catastrophic.

Identifying STINK Bomb
Imagine that you're with a group of friends. You're all laughing and having a good time. Then the unthinkable happens. Yes, someone drops

a STINK bomb, and the conversation shifts immediately. It might go something like this: (laughing....) (more laughing....) Josh lights the fuse to the STINK bomb and says, "Hey, did any of you see Madison's new haircut?" Hannah sets the STINK bomb off by saying, "Man, what a hideous haircut." Aidan adds another STINK bomb, "It fits her just right. She is such a loser!" Ryan lights another STINK bomb by saying, "Yea, I know what you mean. The other day Madison was coming out the bathroom, and she had toilet paper stuck to her shoe. When I pointed it out, she gave me a nasty look. See if I help her anymore!" The conversation will continue down this path until someone can diffuse all the awful STINK bombs.

Ingredients of a STINK Bomb

STINK bombs have a number of ingredients. The first one is poor self-esteem. If you think about it, it makes perfect sense. Why would someone feel the need to say something negative about a person if they felt really good about themselves? You see, people drop STINK bombs as a way to disguise their own STINK.

ANOTHER MAJOR INGREDIENT OF A STINK BOMB IS STINKIN' THINKIN'.

Yes, STINKIN' THINKIN' is always present when a STINK bomb explodes. If you eliminate negative thinking, you would be in a much better place to be able to diffuse it. When you change STINKIN' THINKIN' to positive thinking, it acts as a shield and keeps the STINK bomb SMELL from getting to you. It takes practice, but keeping a positive outlook about everyone and everything is the first step in avoiding a STINK bomb.

There are a number of other ingredients in a STINK bomb. Some are worry, guilt, fear, jealously, blame, hate, hurt, anger, and shame. These are just a few of the negative emotions that set up just the right ingredients for a STINK bomb to ignite.

Diffusing a STINK Bomb

Now that you have an idea about how a STINK bomb operates, you're ready to learn how to properly diffuse one. If not done properly, you can actually create more STINK bombs, so be careful.

People really need to have more compassion for others. This is one of the main elements used to diffuse a STINK Bomb. When you're in a group, small or large, notice when someone makes a negative comment about someone else. Once you start noticing when the STINK bomb's fuse is lit, you can quickly diffuse it without having the STINKIN' explosion.

After you realize that a STINK bomb has been lit, see the situation with compassion. Take just a moment and think about how it would feel if someone was saying something negative about you. When you see the situation with compassion, it's easier to diffuse the STINK bomb. You have to see with compassion for both sides. Did the person who ignited the STINK bomb get hurt by the person they're talking about? Is there a history involved that could backfire if you try to diffuse it?

Once you see the situation from both sides, it's time to start diffusing. With the careful precision of a surgeon, you need to pick apart the ingredients that ignited it. If the person is angry, frustrated or jealous, you can use those feelings to help diffuse the STINK bomb. You do this by acknowledging where they are coming from before trying to diffuse the STINK bomb.

For example, you are having lunch with Sarah. You and Sarah have a friend named Emily. Sarah is very jealous of Emily because Emily gets everything she wants. Now, Sarah is unhappy because Emily just got a video game that you know Sarah has wanted for weeks. During lunch Sarah lights the fuse to a STINK bomb: "That Emily went out and got that game just to spite me. She can be so mean!" Now, you can either let the STINK bomb explode and add something negative, or you can diffuse it. Let's say that you choose to diffuse it. You could say, "You know, Sarah, I can understand where you're coming from. It probably doesn't feel very good to not be able to get that game for yourself. But why not look at this from a different point of view? Now you have a friend who has it, and you can go over to her house and play the game anytime you like. Just think, if she didn't have the game, you wouldn't be able to play it at all."

This strategy even works in a large group where there may be more than one person feeling the effects of STINKIN' THINKIN'. To properly diffuse a STINK bomb in a large group, you still need to see the situation with compassion from both points of view. Simply saying something nice about the person each time someone in the group says something negative may be enough. In most cases, this will diffuse the STINK bomb because it's hard for some people to come back with another negative response when you've said a positive one. However, there are occasions where diffusing a STINK bomb creates a chain reaction of STINK bombs. These super bombs are called Atomic STINK bombs because they create a massive cloud of STINK and are very serious if you're in close proximity.

Atomic STINK Bombs

Atomic STINK bombs typically occur in larger groups. They can be identified as such when there's a lot of negative emotion coming from many people. Diffusing these STINK bombs is very, very difficult. Some atomic STINK bombs cannot be diffused because when emotions are high, intelligence is low. This means that when you try to use common sense and compassion to diffuse an atomic STINK bomb, it can actually backfire on you.

Sugar

Sugar used to ignite STINK bombs with her gossip but now teaches others how to diffuse them.

When emotions are high enough, trying to diffuse an Atomic STINK bomb only adds fuel to the fire. In these situations, first try to change the subject. Adding something positive about that person may very well make the situation much worse. If for some reason the group continues the negative talk about the person, simply walk away. You can make up an excuse to leave, such as needing to run to the restroom or run an errand. If you're in a situation where you can't leave, don't add anything to the conversation even if someone asks you to. Periodically trying to change the subject may be your only solution.

One cool thing about STINK bombs is that the SMELL quickly goes away after they are diffused. All you have to do is be aware when someone lights a STINK bomb. Avoid adding fuel to the fire. Instead, use compassion and see both points of view without taking sides in the process.

STINKIN' EXERCISE:
BUILDING A STINK BOMB SHELTER

This exercise is a fun way to discover how to diffuse STINK bombs. No one likes it when others gossip about them behind their backs. Now you have a tool to help identify and diffuse these situations. Once you have successfully diffused a STINK bomb, you'll feel really good about yourself. Your positive energy will rise, as will the energy of all those involved in the conversation.

For this exercise you will need the following:

- a poster board
- a red marker
- scissors
- glue

- a 3" x 5" index card
- a pencil

Step by Step Instructions

STEP 1: Using your pencil, draw 20 matchsticks on your poster board. Or, you can print out twenty copies of a matchstick picture like the one above and glue them to the poster board.

STEP 2: Color the tips of the matchsticks with your red marker, if the matchsticks aren't printed in color.

STEP 3: Cut the 20 matchsticks out of the poster board. The poster board will be thick enough to hold up throughout the day.

STEP 4: Start your day with the 20 paper matchsticks in your pocket, purse or backpack.

STEP 5: When you spot a STINK bomb (someone saying something negative about another person) immediately try to diffuse it. See it from both sides, and either say something nice about the victim or try to change the subject.

STEP 6: If you were able to diffuse the situation, take one of the paper matches and place it in the your other pocket or in another pocket in your purse or backpack.

STEP 7: If the speaker continues adding more negative comments or someone else chimes in, the STINK bomb has gone off! Take one of the paper matches, tear it in half, and then place it in the other pocket or in a different location in your purse.

STEP 8: Each night, count the number of diffused as well as ignited STINK bombs. Pull out the poster board and make the following headers and marks:

Day	Stink Bombs	Ignited	Diffused
1			
2			
3			
4			

STEP 9: Repeat for 4 days

Your goal is to diffuse more STINK bombs than those that ignite. When you accomplish this feat four times in a row (that is 16 days total), you have graduated to the STINK Bomb Squad Academy! Send an email to: stinkbombs@idontstink.com and you will be sent an electronic STINK Bomb Academy patch!

Expected Results

The first time you try to diffuse a STINK bomb, it might be awkward and difficult, but the more you try it, the easier it gets. You might not experience much success in the first couple of days, but by the third and fourth day the exercise gets easier and is actually quite fun. Continue to repeat the exercise until you have properly diffused more STINK bombs than were ignited.

Tips for a Successful Exercise

- For this exercise, you have to become aware of what others are saying.
- Try listening instead of talking in group discussions. Listen as though you are taking notes in a classroom so you can become aware of potential STINK bombs.
- Don't get discouraged if you can't diffuse a STINK bomb on your first try.
- Lots of STINK bombs are ignited every day. Use your awareness to identify them.
- Listen for negative words in conversations, such as mean, jerk, loser, goofy, stupid, etc..... Anytime someone describes someone else using a negative word, a stink bomb is being lit.
- Remember that any time someone says something negative to you, try not to add to the discussion unless you're trying to diffuse the STINK bomb.
- Remain neutral when trying to diffuse a STINK bomb. Don't attempt to take sides, no matter how appealing it might be.

The STINKIN' Summary

- STINK bombs are lit when someone brings up something negative about someone else.
- STINK bombs cause a serious STINK.
- Once deployed, STINK bombs can attract STINKIN' people with negative attitudes.
- The proper way to diffuse a STINK bomb is to see the situation with compassion for both sides.
- STINK bombs contain ingredients such as poor self-esteem, STINKIN'THINKIN', worry, frustration, guilt, fear, blame, hate, hurt, shame, anger, and jealously.
- Sometimes just changing the subject can diffuse a STINK bomb.
- Atomic STINK bombs occur in larger groups and require special handling.

STINK bombs are easy to spot once you know what to look for. Basically, any negative emotion can contain a STINK bomb in it somewhere. You can diffuse a STINK bomb by adding something positive to the conversation or changing the subject altogether.

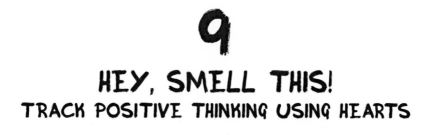

9
HEY, SMELL THIS!
TRACK POSITIVE THINKING USING HEARTS

"Nothing but sweetness can remain when hearts are full of their own sweetness." —William Butler Yeats (Writer, Dramatist, and Poet, 1865–1939)

STINKIN' THINKIN' Translation:
If you SMELL SA-WEET, then everything around you will SMELL SA-WEET!

While negative thoughts STINK, positive thoughts SMELL wonderful. It's your challenge to maintain a SWEET SMELL and then share it with everyone around you. The same way that STINKIN' THINKIN' attracts more STINKIN' thoughts or STINKIN' people with STINKIN' thoughts, SWEET SMELLING thoughts attract more SWEET thoughts and people who SMELL good. Now that's a SWEET combination!

After you take out your STINKIN' trash, you'll notice that you feel better about things. Nothing will seem quite as bad as it did before. You will experience fewer STINKIN' thoughts and more and more SWEET ones! SWEET things only get SWEETER.

ONE WAY TO ELIMINATE STINKIN' THINKIN' IS TO START TRACKING YOUR POSITIVE THINKING.

Tracking positive thinking works just the same as tracking your negative thoughts. Once you become aware of SWEET thinking, you are destined to look for more things to compliment. One of the main goals of positive thinking is to put more focus on what you want, versus what you don't what. This is because

YOU ARE A MAGNET FOR THE VERY THINGS YOU ARE THINKING ABOUT.

Remembering that one phrase will change how you feel, how you react, and how you experience your life.

Do you know someone who has a positive attitude? If you do, pay close attention to what they say, how they say it, and how they react to people with negative attitudes. You'll certainly learn something from them. Ask them questions about how they maintain positivity, and then try your best to duplicate the qualities that feel best for you. If you don't know someone with a positive attitude, do a little research on positive public figures and then read biographical articles or books about them. You can learn a lot about them, including things you can start to imitate. Remember:

THE MORE YOU PRACTICE BEING POSITIVE, THE MORE NATURAL BEING POSITIVE WILL BECOME.

The time has come to replace the STENCH of STINKIN' THINKIN' with a SWEET AROMA of all good things. Here's a SUPER COOL exercise to help you do just that. While this exercise might be slightly more complex than the previous ones, the benefits of it can be life changing.

Rosie

Rosie loves to make other people's days by giving them paper hearts with kind words written on them.

STINKIN' EXERCISE: HEY, SMELL THIS!

The main purpose of positive thinking is to help you feel good about yourself, your family, your community, your country, and the entire planet, for that matter. Once you become aware of STINKIN' THINKIN', you have the opportunity to change it. And a great way to do this is to start tracking your positive thinking—with your nose.

That's right, with your nose. When you attach a SMELL or fragrance to your successes, each time you experience that SMELL it's like you have chalked up another success. Now that is SUPER SA-WEET!

Before you start this exercise, you will need the following materials:

- 1 poster board
- 3 full sheets of construction paper – pick a variety of colors, except red and black
- magazines or pictures (optional)
- seven 3 x 5 index cards (or pieces of paper cut to 3 x 5 size)
- a pen or pencil
- tape or glue
- a nicely-scented marker
- 1 can of air freshener (Pick a fragrance that you LOVE!)

Step 1: The Hearts

The first step of this exercise is to cut out three very large hearts from the three sheets of construction paper. Use the entire size of the construction paper. Each heart will represent a different theme: 1) tracking your SWEET SMELLING thoughts, 2) items you collected that reinforce your SWEET thoughts, and 3) positive SWEET emotions that you experience as a result of tracking your SWEET SMELLING thoughts. Now label the three hearts:

1. "SWEET SMELLING Thoughts"
2. "I Attracted…."
3. "SWEET Emotions"

Step 2: The Poster

Write **"I SMELL Good!"** at the top of the poster board. Tape or glue the hearts on the poster board wherever you like. In the blank areas of the poster board between the hearts, fill in the space with things you would like in your life. You can cut out pictures from magazines or use real pictures, you can draw your own pictures or cartoons, you can use words, letters, numbers, etc. Those pictures or drawings should represent the positive emotions you would like to experience, like love, happiness, joy, peace, courage, and gratitude.

Step 3: Daily Exercise

In the morning, take out one of the seven index cards and carry it with you all day. It doesn't matter where you go or what you do, just carry it with you all day. Do this every day for the next week. **Every time a single SWEET SMELLIN' thought pops up, say "Thank you. Ahhh!"** Then make a mark on your index card. This means that you're now tracking your positive SWEET SMELLIN' thoughts. I personally love this exercise, and I'm sure that you will, too. Since what you focus on EX-PANDS, paying attention to SWEET SMELLIN' thoughts brings more SWEET SMELLIN' things to you.

Step 4: Updating Heart #1

At night, first update the heart labeled **"SWEET SMELLING Thoughts"** with the SWEET SMELLIN' marks from the day. Start by spraying the scent around the board. Take a nice breath and say, **"I SMELL GOOD!"** and then write the date and the number of marks for the day. An example would be: April 19 – 8, April 20 – 13, April 21 – 18.

Step 5: Updating Heart #2

Second, update the heart labeled **"I Attracted…."** if any items in the blank spaces have shown up in your life. Take another whiff of the scent and say, **"I SMELL GOOD!"** For example, if you listed a fresh new set of markers in the spaces between the hearts and you received one today, then "move" it from the blank spaces to the heart. Do this by drawing an arrow and then either drawing another picture in the heart or simply spelling out what you got.

Step 6: Updating Heart #3

Third, update the heart labeled **"SWEET Emotions"** if you had any really good feelings during the day. Notice the wonderful fragrance of the air freshener again and say, **"I SMELL GOOD!"** If your SWEET emotions are listed in the blank spaces on the poster board, "move" them to the SWEET Emotions heart as described above in Step 6. SWEET emotions are feelings such as happiness, joy, peace, love, excitement, acceptance, bliss, hope, and pleasure.

Repeat steps 4, 5, and 6 every day for seven days.

Step 7: Final Step
Show your poster to your friends, family members, or anyone you would like to see it. Before you tell them what you are doing, preface it by saying, "I SMELL GOOD!" Then explain your new SWEET SMELLIN' poster.

I have one note of caution. Do not attempt this exercise until you have taken out your STINKIN' trash. If you have a whole lot of STINKIN' thoughts and they are not addressed, this exercise will not work very well. It's best to do the Take Out Your STINKIN' Trash exercise first, and then wait a week to do this exercise as you contemplate the results of the first one.

Expected Results
"Hey, SMELL This!" exercise is very, very powerful. The "Take Out Your STINKIN' Trash" exercise brought awareness of your STINKIN' thoughts, and this one will bring awareness to your SWEET SMELLIN' thoughts. Remember, what you focus on EXPANDS, so this exercise is the first one that will allow you to start bringing SWEET things to you. The "Take Out Your STINKIN' Trash" exercise is really just a "deletion" tool and makes you aware of how many negative things you think of during the day. This exercise is more of an "addition" tool because you will start to attract SWEET things as a result of your SWEET thinking practice.

Once you have completed updating each of the hearts for a week, either continue working on it or start a new one. The choice is yours.

Tips for a Successful Exercise

- Take your time on this exercise. There's no rush. Plus, the more time you spend identifying what you want, the better the exercise will turn out.
- Don't spend all your time making the hearts pretty. Spend most of your time deciding what you desire.
- Remember, the goal of this exercise is to discover all the SWEET things in your life already, so put your focus on that for this week.
- If a negative thought comes up, just throw it into the STINKIN' trash.
- Once the exercise is completed, share the successes with someone you love. That's a great way to relive the success, and it may inspire them to think positively too. After all, positive thinking is as contagious as STINKIN' THINKIN'.
- You can pick a friend to do the exercise with you. If you do, build all the material together, but practice the exercise daily by yourself.

The STINKIN' Summary

- Positive thinking smells SA-WEET.
- Tracking positive thinking is one way to eliminate STINK-IN' THINKIN'.
- You attract what you focus on.
- Identify and imitate someone who is positive most of the time.
- Linking a fragrance you love to your successes will breed more successes.
- Share your SWEET successes with others around you.

Positive thoughts SMELL SWEET, and you want to attract more of them to you. Since what you FOCUS on EXPANDS, there's no better way to start attracting SWEET things in your life than to place all your attention on what is good. When you do this, more of what you want and love will start showing up.

It's easy to get back into a STINK mode if you're not careful. To help you keep your STINK out, practice the "Hey, SMELL This!" exercise regularly. After a week of doing the exercise, reflect on all the SWEET things that showed up in your life.

10

HOW TO DEAL WITH OTHER STINKIN' PEOPLE
FORGIVE NEGATIVE THINKING PEOPLE

"Forgiveness is the fragrance that the violet sheds on the heel that has crushed it."
—Mark Twain (Humorist, Writer, and Lecturer, 1835–1910)

STINKIN'THINKIN'Translation:
Unforgiveness is like stepping in something that STINKS and blaming your shoes.

When you have completed the "Take Out Your STINKIN' Trash" and "Hey, SMELL This!" exercises, you might feel compelled to help other STINKIN' people. A word of caution here: When you are focused on helping other STINKIN' people, you take the focus off your own SWEET thoughts and actions. Another issue is that

WHILE YOU MAY SMELL THE STINKIN' PEOPLE, THEY MAY NOT KNOW THAT THEY STINK AT ALL.

Or they may know that they STINK but not care. Only offer to help STINKIN' people when they want help.

It's said that when the student is ready, the teacher will come. This applies to STINKIN' people also. Sometimes the process to CLEANSE yourself can take quite a bit of time. So always be patient with yourself as well as with others when you are attempting to help them. Their past and their willingness to change the present will have a direct impact on how long this process may take.

If you feel that you SMELL good enough to help others, certainly do so. But realize that

THE BEST WAY TO HELP OTHER STINKIN' PEOPLE IS TO HELP YOUR SWEET SELF FIRST. AND THEN SET A SWEET EXAMPLE.

Be an example of how you hope others can be. As you develop your own SWEET AROMA, others will be attracted to you. They may be your STINKIN' friends, or they may be folks who have a nice SWEET AROMA themselves. Either way, as they start to notice the changes in your life, they will get curious. They will ask you what you're doing and when they do, share with them the lessons you've learned. Don't share this information until you detect some curiosity from others. Then simply tell them "I Don't STINK! because I am choosing to SMELL good." You can then tell them about this book and/or the website, www.idonts-tink.com, and they can find out if they STINK by taking the STINKIN' quiz, just like you did.

At some point during the work on your own STINKIN' THINKIN', you'll discover that you want to do more to make a difference in other STINKIN' people's lives. One way to super charge your SWEET ARO-MA is to practice something that most people don't ever do: forgiving. Forgiveness of other STINKIN' people will help you in more ways than can be mentioned here.

Please understand that if you truly want to help other STINKIN' people, there are two simple ways to help. One is by helping yourself. Lead by example and tell them how you got your STINK out. The second way is accomplished through the simple act of forgiveness.

FORGIVENESS OF BOTH YOURSELF AND OF OTHERS IS THE KEY TO PEACE, HAPPINESS, AND JOY.

There is an entire section on forgiveness in the book *7 Days to Inner Peace: The Building Blocks of Awareness,* and it includes a very unique "Forgiveness Bucket" exercise that is both fun and easy. Here is a summary for you to get started. First you designate 4 buckets:

Bucket #1: I Don't Want to Forgive
Bucket #2: I Don't Know How to Forgive
Bucket #3: I Want to Forgive
Bucket #4: I Can and Will Forgive

First you have to figure out whom you need to forgive. Then the idea is to determine which bucket each STINKIN' person fits into, and then put them in the bucket. As you practice forgiveness, when you start to feel even the slightest change in the way you look at them, move them to the next bucket until they make it into Bucket #4.

To move STINKIN' people to other buckets, an easy thing to do is to say an affirmation. Start by saying, "I forgive _____ (name). And I forgive myself." Just say that over and over each day as many times as you can during the day. After a while, you will feel a difference in how you look at them. That's the time to move them to the next bucket. Continue to do this until the STINKIN' people are no longer in those heavy buckets of un-forgiveness that you tote around in your daily life.

One important note is to

REMEMBER TO FORGIVE YOURSELF FOR ANY STINK MODE YOU GOT YOURSELF INTO.

A lot of people aren't aware of how negatively they talk, either *to* themselves or *about* themselves. They may be using the word *can't* often in their vocabulary or stating their negativity in the form of affirmations, like, "I am so stupid!" or any other negative comment about yourself. Always forgive yourself first, always think positively about yourself and your abilities, and then you will have the power to help other STINKIN' people.

You basically have three ways to help other STINKIN' people.

1. You can tell them about the work you are doing when the STINKIN' person asks about the changes in you.
2. You can set a SWEET-smelling example.
3. You can forgive the STINKIN' person. The longer you SMELL GOOD, the more you'll attract the SWEET AROMA of others.

STINKIN' EXERCISE: STINK ROCKS FOR STINKIN' PEOPLE

Since forgiveness is such an important tool to help any STINK-IN' person, this exercise focuses on forgiving. When you forgive someone, you give an incredible gift to the world and to yourself. And when you practice it regularly, you'll feel the weight of un-forgiveness lifted from your shoulders.

Sweetie
Sweetie is very forgiving of others and practices with STINK rocks every day.

This exercise will teach you the power of forgiveness by using awareness, compassion, love, and gratitude. Now that is one SWEET combination!

Before you start this exercise, you will need the following items:

- 4 rocks – each one a different size. One large one about the size of a baseball, one about the size of a golf ball, one the size of a quarter, and one the size of a dime.
- 4 resealable sandwich baggies
- 1 balloon
- 1 white poster board
- a picture of the person you choose to forgive
- a pen or pencil
- a set of markers

First, take out the poster board and draw a mountain on it. On the mountain, write the word "forgiveness" in very large letters. Decorate the mountain as much as you like; just make sure that you can see the word "forgiveness" from all the way across the room. On the left side of the poster board, draw a barren, rocky terrain with lots of brown, gray, and tan colors. Also, draw some rain clouds on the left side of the mountain. On the right side of the mountain, draw a clear sky with sunlight, animals, a stream, and anything bright and cheery, using brightly colored markers. Draw lots of plants, flowers, grass, trees, etc. You should be able to quickly see the differences between the two sides of the mountain.

Mark six evenly placed checkpoints on the left side of the mountain. Mark a seventh checkpoint just past the peak of the mountain.

This exercise will take seven days to complete. Your job is to identify several people in your life that you need to forgive. These could be family members, friends, teachers, etc. A lot of times those people are folks you don't like or whom you get angry about when just thinking their names. Make the list on the clean sheet of paper, writing their names across the top of the page. Choose one person from the list you will work on for all seven days of this exercise. Then you will start the exercise again with another name from the list.

Now it's time to start the exercise. Again, pick only one person to start the exercise with. Grab the dime-sized STINK rock and put the other STINK rocks aside for now.

Day 1: Awareness
Start your day by picking up the dime-sized STINK rock and saying the following: "I forgive you, _____ (name), and I forgive myself." Carry the rock with you as much as you can throughout the day. Each time you feel or see the rock, think of the word "awareness" as if it were written on the rock itself. Then imagine the person you need to forgive holding the rock. At night, draw a picture of a smiley face or checkmark on the mountain at the first checkpoint.

Day 2: Awareness
Repeat the Day 1 exercise. Then at night, draw another smiley face or

checkmark on the mountain at the second checkpoint.

Day 3: Compassion

Start the third day by picking up the quarter-sized STINK rock and saying the following: "I forgive you, _____ (name), and I forgive myself." Carry the bigger rock with you as much as you can. Each time you feel or see the rock, think of the words "awareness" and "compassion" as if they were written on the rock itself. Then imagine the person you need to forgive holding the rock. Draw a smiley face or checkmark on the mountain at the third checkpoint.

Day 4: Compassion

Repeat the Day 3 exercise. This time, draw a picture of that person on the mountain at the fourth checkpoint.

Day 5: Love

Today, start your day by picking up the golf ball-sized STINK rock and saying the following: "I forgive you, _____ (name), and I forgive myself." Carry the rock with you as much as you can. Each time you feel or see the rock, think of the words "awareness," "compassion," and "love" as though they were written on the rock itself. Then imagine the person holding the rock. Draw a smiley face or checkmark on the mountain at the fifth checkpoint.

Day 6: Gratitude

Start day six by picking up the baseball-sized STINK rock and saying the following, "I forgive you, _____ (name), and I forgive myself." Then carry the rock with you as much as you can throughout the day. Each time you feel or see the rock, think of the words "awareness," "compassion," "love," and "gratitude." Then imagine the person you need to forgive holding the rock. Draw a smiley face or checkmark on the mountain at the sixth checkpoint.

Day 7: Forgiveness

Start your day by blowing up the balloon to the size of a golf ball. Say the following: "I forgive you, _____ (name), and I forgive myself." Carry the balloon with you all day. Each time you feel or see the balloon, think of the word "forgiveness" as if it were written on the balloon. Then imagine the person you need to forgive holding the balloon. Draw a smiley face or checkmark on the mountain at the seventh checkpoint, and put a photo of the person you just forgave on the bright, colorful side of the mountain.

Expected Results

The key components of forgiveness are awareness, compassion, love, and gratitude. You'll notice that due to the increasing weight of the STINK rocks, your task is the hardest near the top of the mountain. That's the point where a lot of people give up because it's the hardest. You'll also notice that, unlike the rocks in the exercise, you carry the weight of something left unforgiven 24 hours a day, seven days a week. It's time to lighten your load. After seven days of working on forgiveness, you'll feel different from when you started. Lighter. Freer. Your goal is to move any person presenting you with an opportunity for forgiveness from one side of the mountain to the other. The left side of the mountain represents unforgiveness and sadness, while the right side of the mountain represents the beauty and grace of forgiveness and peace.

Tips for a Successful Exercise

- When drawing your poster, be sure to make the right side as colorful as possible. This side represents your ultimate goal and should be beautiful.
- The left side of the poster should be dark, tan, brown, gray, etc. This is where you are if you haven't forgiven.
- On your first try, pick a person you feel is the easiest to forgive. You can work on the other ones later.
- Decide to be dedicated to carrying the rocks with you as much as you can during the day. At the very least, they should be carried three hours.

- Don't forget to add the part about forgiving yourself. That represents the complete cycle of forgiveness.
- Notice how light the balloon is compared to the STINK rocks. The STINK rocks represent the burden you carry with you all the time while carrying unforgiving thoughts.

The STINKIN' Summary

- Always help yourself first before attempting to help other STINKIN' people.
- STINKIN' people may not know that they STINK.
- Other SWEET people will be attracted to you when you get rid of STINKIN' THINKIN'.
- Forgiveness is an important factor when helping other STINKIN' people.

As you start raising your awareness of your STINKIN' thoughts and tracking your SWEET SMELLIN' ones, you might be inclined to start helping other STINKIN' people. This is a wonderful thing to do. But beware, helping others can cause you to stop working on your own STINKIN' self, and you may face a struggle when others resist your help. Help them when they are curious about how you've changed or ask you for help. In the meantime, continue raising your SWEETNESS to higher and higher heights.

II
WATCH OUT FOR STINK BUGS
SPOTTING AND AVOIDING NEGATIVE PEOPLE

"Smell is a potent wizard that transports you across thousands of miles and all the years you have lived." —Helen Keller
(Author and Educator who was blind and deaf, 1880–1968)

STINKIN' THINKIN' Translation:
Remain unaware of your STINK, and you
will emit a STENCH that will last forever!

To keep yourself STINK-FREE, you need to learn how to spot a STINK bug. A STINK bug is any type of foul-SMELLING insect. In this book they represent any person whose main way of thinking, either by choice or by their lack of awareness, is STINKIN' THINKIN'.

STINK bugs can be pretty easy to spot. You just have to follow your nose, or in this case, your gut. Your gut, or intuition, will tell you when you are around STINK bugs. Trust your gut when it subtly tells you, "Don't say anything," "Just walk away," or even "Don't go there with them." Remember, any time you become aware of your STINKIN' THINKIN', you are one step closer to SMELLING SWEET, and it will be much easier to spot a STINK bug. Since awareness is key, be sure to "Take out your STINKIN' Trash" regularly and don't let it build up.

It can be quite embarrassing when someone in your group of friends SMELLS up the place. It's really bad when someone walks up and says, "Hey, what STINKS?" Now when you hear this, it'll have a whole different meaning, won't it? Chances are, if you're around other STINK-IN' people, you're getting a hint of STINKINESS from one of those STINK bugs.

The best way to spot STINK bugs is to find a way to

KEEP STINKIN' THINKIN' FROM CONTROLLING YOUR THOUGHTS.

Once you clear away your own STINKIN' THINKIN', awareness of any STINK bugs around you naturally follows. But beware. Being close to STINK bugs will make it much harder for you to fight your STINK-IN' thoughts. Yes, you still will occasionally have a STINKIN' thought. Everyone does. But once you commit to positivity and do the exercises in this book, you'll be well on your way to SMELLING GOOD. And when you SMELL GOOD, it's really easy to spot a STINK bug.

STINK bugs aren't just regular STINKIN' people. They are people who don't mind SMELLING awful and like to wallow in negativity, usually offering negative responses to anything you say. You have to be careful around them, because their SMELL can be contagious.

STINK BUGS CAN INFECT YOU WITH STENCH

without you even knowing it! To spot a STINK bug, use your newfound awareness and listen to what others are saying.

Think about it for a minute. Have you ever given someone a compliment or done something nice for them, only to have them respond with something mean or hurtful? This is considered the larvae stage of a STINK bug. If not treated properly, a full metamorphosis will transform them into a full-fledged STINK bug.

Now comes the hard part. What happens when you're not able to spot the STINK bug? Good question. Not all STINK bugs are alike. Each one has its own unique SMELL. Some talk your head off, constantly complaining about other STINKIN' people. Others will say absolutely nothing. The quiet STINK bugs can be the deadliest. They keep all their STINKIN' trash bottled up, and when you least expect it, there's a massive STINKIN' explosion. And if you are close by, you are hit with the RANCID STENCH of the percussive STINKIN' blast. You'll find that it's very difficult to wash out that STENCH because it's so strong.

To spot these STINK bugs, use your awareness, intuition, and gut. And if your friends are STINK bugs, you don't *have* to find all new friends, but you *do* have to make a choice. Some people choose to ignore the STINK bugs and stay friends with them anyway. While that may be an option for some of you, others might want to consider ways to help their STINKIN' friends, as discussed in the previous chapter. If you can't help them, though, it might be time to break off the friendship. Why? Because STINKIN' THINKIN' is contagious, and once you've worked hard to get rid of your STINKIN' THINKIN', you don't want to get it back. Remember to look for friends who support you and challenge you to become a better person. That's what a true friend is anyway, isn't it?

ONE STINKIN' EXPLOSION FROM A STINK BUG CAN HAVE DEVASTATING EFFECTS ON YOUR FRIENDSHIP.

Twiggy
Twiggy watches out for STINK bugs everywhere she goes because she doesn't want their STENCH to get on her.

If you always try to *be* the kind of friend you want to have yourself, you'll attract more positive friends than negative ones.

STINKIN' EXERCISE:
USING A STINK BUG SHIELD

Have you ever seen a bug shield on a car? That's the shield that deflects bugs, keeping them from spattering all over your windshield and making it hard to see the road through all the guts and stuff. YUCK! This exercise works the same way. It keeps STINK bugs from impairing your ability to see things clearly. Some STINK bugs are pretty clever and can twist your vision without you even knowing it. This exercise was developed to provide you with the necessary tools to not only *spot* a STINK bug, but to also to develop listening skills that are necessary to find STINK bugs.

For this exercise, you will need the following items:

- 1 white poster board
- a set of markers

- three 3 x 5 index cards (or pieces of paper cut to 3 x 5 size)
- a pen or pencil

First, take out your poster board and draw a car windshield on it. Basically, all you have to do is draw the outline. Above the windshield, write the words, "STINK Bug Shield." Below the windshield, write, "Day 1 _____ Day 2 _____ Day 3 _____" Space them evenly across the bottom of the poster.

This will be a three-day exercise. On the first day, carry a 3" x 5" index card with you, along with your pen or pencil. Your job is to spot as many STINK bugs as you can. To do this, you'll have to listen to what others are saying.

Day 1: Listen
On the first day, just listen for STINK bugs. Listen for negative words. If you hear negative words being said, put a mark on your 3" x 5" index card. Only one mark per person, no matter how many negative words they use. At the end of the day, add up the marks and write the total under "Day 1 _____" on your poster. Using black, red, yellow, and brown markers, draw splattered bugs in the left third of your STINK bug shield equal to the number you encountered on "Day 1 _____."

Day 2: Ask
Today, talk to as many people as you can. Ask them the following question: "How are you doing?" Then, listen to their responses. If you notice negative words in their responses, mark your index card. You can even use the telephone to talk to friends and family. Remember to ask the question before you talk about anything else. At the end of the day, write the total under "Day 2 _____" on your poster. Using black, red, and green markers, draw splattered bugs in the center third of your STINK bug shield equal to the number for "Day 2 _____."

Day 3: Positive Suggestion
Today, your exercise is to talk to as many people as you can, just like day

two. This time, though, ask, "What's making you happy today?" If you notice negative words in their responses, mark your index card. At the end of the day, write the total under "Day 3 _____" on your poster. With black, red, brown, and yellow markers, draw splattered bugs in the right third on your STINK bug shield equal to the number for "Day 3 ____."

Expected Results

Results will vary greatly on this exercise. You might have a hard time recognizing negative responses at first. This is because your awareness has not been fully developed yet. The main idea of the exercise is to show you that when you say something positive, more people will respond in a positive manner. This means that you will probably have more marks on days 1 and 2 than on day 3. What can you deduce from these results? That's right! If *you're* positive, lots of times the people around you are more positive.

Tips for a Successful Exercise

- On Day 1, act as though you're a detective. Be very quiet and just focus all your senses on listening.
- Just for fun, on Day 3, ask the STINK bugs identified during Day 2 what's making them happy. See if there's a change in their response.
- Name the splattered STINK bugs if you like. Poor Matt! He really went SPLAT!
- If your STINK bug windshield is completely filled up, do the exercise "Take out your STINKIN' Trash" again to make sure you're not starting to become a STINK bug yourself.
- Try the exercise with just your friends.
- Try the exercise next time you have a family reunion or a large family gathering but shorten it to just one day.

The STINKIN' Summary

- A STINK bug is any person whose thinking is mostly negative.
- Always use your gut when determining if someone is a STINK bug.
- Be careful when you're around quiet STINK bugs.
- STINK bugs can infect you with their STENCH if you're not careful.
- Look for friends who will support you.

Some STINK bugs are easy to spot, but some can be very difficult to root out. When you put up your STINK bug shield, you'll be able to decide for yourself who is a STINK bug and who is not. Once a STINK bug is identified, be sure help to them by setting a positive example.

12

HELP! I JUST MADE A STINK!
STINK EPISODES LASTING TOO LONG

*"Positive thinking will let you do
everything better than negative thinking will."*
—Zig Ziglar (Motivational Speaker and Author, 1926-2012)

STINKIN' THINKIN' Translation:
If your THINKIN' STINKS, everything you do will STINK! And if
your THINKIN' is SWEET, everything you do will smell SA-WEET.

STINKIN' THINKIN' can happen to anyone, anywhere, at any time. It doesn't matter your age or your shoe size. No one is immune, and you can't run and hide from it. Sometimes STINKIN' THINKIN' sneaks up on you, and you aren't aware that it's about to wreak havoc on everything in your life.

EVEN THE MOST POSITIVE PEOPLE HAVE TO DEAL WITH STINKIN' THINKIN'.

Sometimes they even struggle. However, they typically tend to get themselves out of their own STINK modes by using tools they've developed to maintain their positive attitude. So what happens to the majority of people who haven't developed any tools on their own to deal with their STINKIN' THINKIN'? That's the easy part! This book is filled with some SWEET tools they can use to change even the STINKIEST THINKIN' ever. The supporting website for this book, www.idontstink. com, contains a wealth of information on how to get rid of STINKIN' THINKIN'—and even more tools.

When you let STINKIN' THINKIN' go unattended, it can cause even the SWEETEST person to do STINKIN' things. Also, just

BECOMING AWARE OF STINKIN' THINKIN' WON'T MAKE IT GO AWAY.

You have to use your awareness to identify it and then *change* it. Do you know the definition of insanity? It's doing the same thing over and over again while expecting different results.

IF YOU DON'T EVER DO SOMETHING DIFFERENT, NOTHING WILL EVER CHANGE.

The cool part is that when you attempt something different, even if it doesn't work, you've taken a huge step in the right direction, and your attitude about STINKIN' THINKIN' will start to change.

It's amazing what one little STINK episode can do to you and others who are a part of it. It takes only

ONE BAD CHOICE TO CAUSE PEOPLE TO REGRET THEIR ACTIONS FOR A LIFETIME.

And you don't want to go there, my friend. Here's a story about a STINKIN' episode I had when I was nine years old. It clearly shows you how one STINKIN' thought led to life-long regret – that is, until I learned to forgive myself. I do not excuse this type of behavior. This was a learning opportunity for me, and I share it as an example of what NOT to do.

THE STINKIN' SQUIRT STORY

When I was nine years old, baseball was my favorite sport. My favorite major league baseball player was George Brett of the Kansas City Royals. He played third base, so I played third base. He wore number five, so I wore number five. He was a major leaguer, so my goals were to become a major leaguer, too.

From early spring until the end of summer, I would play baseball every single day. When we weren't having a baseball game or practice, I practiced at home using something called a "pitchback." A pitchback is a tightly woven net that springs the ball back to the person who threw the ball into it. It has a square in the middle to designate the strike zone so that players can practice control. I typically practiced at least two hours a day—and sometimes as many as 4 hours. Each season I wore out at least two pitchbacks.

Not only was I a pretty good third baseman, I was a very accurate pitcher. After we practiced several weeks, I was one of the two main pitchers our coach used to start games. We played two games a week. I would pitch one game, and another guy twice my size would pitch the other. I didn't have an over-powering fastball, just a knack for placing the ball precisely where I wanted it most of the time. As a result, I rarely ever walked anyone.

Lastly, before I get to the STINKIN' story, I learned at a very early age how to use positive thinking and visualization in sports. I would picture the ball in the catcher's mitt before I even started my windup. The game where STINKIN' THINKIN' came into play for me was in the twelfth game of the season. I had five wins and zero loses under my belt, and I felt that I could never lose. I was pretty full of myself, thinking I was the greatest nine year old ever to play the game! You could say that was the first hint of my STINKIN' THINKIN'.

We were the home team for this twelfth game of the season, so I was on the mound doing my warm-up tosses. But instead of thinking about pitching a good game, all I could think about was going 6-0 and being undefeated for the season. That would surely mean I would be selected for the all-star team!

But the season changed for me in an instant. As I watched the first batter step up to the plate, my STINKIN' THINKIN' started. *That little squirt is the shortest baseball player in the league,* I thought. To make matters worse, he hunched down and stuck his elbow into the strike zone. He couldn't have been much more than 24 inches tall hunched over like that. I was agitated before I even delivered the first pitch of the game. And that moment set the stage for a miserable game for me.

The first pitch I threw was a perfect strike, or at least that's how I saw it. The catcher didn't move his mitt at all. But the umpire called it a ball. Next pitch: ball two. Then ball three and ball four. "Take your base!" the umpire told the batter. I was very angry that I had walked the leadoff hitter and that my game had started off so badly. And the game went downhill from there.

The next time the small batter came up to the plate, I had the same results. I was fuming now and arguing with the umpire over the call of balls and strikes. Any player knows that arguing with the umpire won't help you, but I did it anyway. At that point, all borderline calls seemed to be going in the other team's favor, which only fueled my STINKIN' THINKIN' even more. I thought to myself, *Everybody's out to get me today. What did I do to deserve this?*

The small batter's third at bat went just as the previous two had. Four pitches. Four balls. If you haven't figured it out by now, my team was losing. My perfect season was in serious jeopardy, and I wasn't helping at all when it was my turn to bat either. I ended up hitless and struck out several times, which was rare for me. My STINKIN' THINKIN' played the major roll because I just couldn't shake that STINKIN' squirt!

One thing that I learned early in the season was to intimidate the batter. You may not believe me, but I actually learned this from my mom. She told me that before throwing my first pitch of the game, I should always stare at the batter until I saw him look away. Then she told me to send the first pitch sailing high and tight. In other words, near his chest and head. Yeah, she really told me that. And since I had pinpoint accuracy, I could get away with it without ever hitting a batter. I was good at it, and the strikeouts followed.

So when that STINKIN' squirt —Yes, that's exactly what I thought of him! —came up to his fourth and final at bat, my STINKIN' THINKIN' made me do something I have regretted ever since. He stepped into the batter's box and stuck that left elbow way out, just like he'd done the other three times. My STINKIN' THINKIN' told me, *Heck, you might as well just hit him since you're going to walk him again, anyway.*

When he came up to bat, he stuck that left elbow right into the strike zone again. I stared at him for a long time first, just like Mom had taught me, and fixed my target on that stupid elbow. I pictured the ball hitting it. Then I threw a fastball hard enough that he wouldn't have time to move out of its way.

Sure enough, SMACK!, right on target. I had never hit a batter before, but I'm sad to say that this is exactly what I did. I beaned him. Plunked him right in that elbow.

The kid dropped to the dirt like he'd been hit by a cannon ball and started to cry. His coach ran out, and I didn't even dare look in the stands for his parents. At that moment, I felt worse than I ever had in my entire life.

I know it had to hurt because it caught him right on the end of his elbow and the sound was horrible. The coach called for a bag of ice from the concession stand, and concerned grown-ups helped wrap a bandage around the bag so it would stay on the kid's elbow. When the kid finally got up, it looked like his arm had been amputated. He sniffled all the way to first base and after he touched it, a pinch runner came in for him. My head was hanging so low my nose nearly dragged the ground, and I felt so ashamed.

We went on to lose badly, and I was never quite the same pitcher again after that game. I went on to post a 7-2 record but struggled with my STINKIN' THINKIN' the rest of the season. I started doubting my ability and lost my confidence. I started walking more batters because I didn't ever want to hit another one. Unfortunately, because all my focus was on NOT hitting a batter, the result was that I accidentally hit one in every single game. This was because my attention was on not hitting them rather than on throwing strikes as I did before this STINK episode! When I changed my focus, I quickly lost the pinpoint control I had had for the first five games. Incidentally, I also stopped my intimidation ritual—which was the only good thing to come out of the whole mess.

I tell this story to show you what STINKIN' THINKIN' can turn into if you don't deal with it. Before I even threw that first pitch, I let it talk me into having a lousy, STINKIN' ballgame. STINKIN' THINKIN' tricked me into believing that it was that kid's fault, not mine. Certainly it wasn't my fault that the kid was so short and stuck his elbow into the strike zone! And it was absolutely not my fault that the umpires were so clueless, right?

Wrong. Just the opposite was true. It was entirely my fault. I let STINKIN' THINKIN' stay in my head. After that game, one STINK-IN' thought led to another, and another, and another, and continued for nearly a year. If I would have only taken a deep breath and let the STINKIN' THINKIN' go, I would have had a much different outcome. I know that for sure. Whether we won the game or not is unimportant. I would have *felt* much better about myself instead of beating myself up with guilt and shame for making such a bad choice.

Luckily, by practicing forgiveness on myself, I was able to let my negative past actions go. In doing so, I felt as if a weight that I was carrying on my shoulders was lifted. Practicing forgiveness really can have that kind of impact.

Another point I want to make is that I put my attention on myself more than the team. Notice the common use of the words "me" and "my" instead of team. As I reached for personal glory and the spotlight, the team definitely suffered. After I started showing my frustration, it was like the floodgates were opened for everyone else on the team. We all started kicking the dirt, arguing with the umpires, with coaches, and with each other. And it all started with my first STINKIN' thought, and then got bombarded with more STINKIN' THINKIN' until it was seriously out of control. How's that for a STINK bomb?

STINKIN' EXERCISE: RECORDING OVER A STINK EPISODE

Since we all have STINK episodes in our lives, it is important to know you can re-record them to get the STINK out. You do this by remaking a movie in your mind of the STINK episode. Once you do this, you will feel better about yourself and will be prepared if a similar STINK moment is presented to you.

Skids

Skids hasn't yet realized that one STINKIN' thought can lead to more and more of them.

For this exercise, you will need the following items:

- 1 pad of paper
- 1 roll of black tape
- an old pair of eyeglasses or a cheap plastic pair from an old costume
- a standard remote control
- a pen or pencil

Step 1: Take the pen and pad of paper and think of a STINK episode you've had. This event is something that causes you guilt and shame each time you think of it.

Step 2: Write down a summary of the event (as if you were watching it on TV) and take notes.

Step 3: Take the old pair of glasses and use the black tape to cover up the lenses.

Step 4: Put the glasses on and sit in a quiet and semi-dark place.

Step 5: Imagine that the glasses are special and magical. They allow you watch the STINK episode in your mind, and they let you edit it while it's playing.

Step 6: With the remote control in one hand, hit the play button to start your STINKIN' movie in your mind.

Step 7: Each time you see something you don't like about the real episode, hit "rewind" or "reverse" and back up to the start of the movie.

Step 8: Hit "record" and watch the event playing out in your mind the way you would have liked it to if you had a chance to do it over again.

Step 9: Imagine there is a "save" button on your remote and select it.

Step 10: On the back of the paper, rewrite your story as you saw it when you were editing it in your mind.

For example, recording over my STINKIN' baseball story might look something like this:

- I hit the "play" button while wearing the magic eyeglasses.
- The first pitch is a ball just as before. I don't like that, so I select the "rewind" button.
- Then I press the "record" button, and I make up a different movie in my mind. This time I see the kid fouling off several pitches during his first at bat, and then he hits the ball to the shortstop and is thrown out at first.
- I click the "fast forward" button to the point when I decided to hit the batter.
- In my mind, I have that awful thought when STINKIN' THINKIN' caused me to make a bad decision.
- I press the "record" button on the remote, and I "edit" the video again. This time when I have that STINKIN' thought, I step off the mound and take a minute to shake it off. Then I step back up onto the pitcher's mound and visualize throwing a perfect strike. I do, and the kid pops it up to the first baseman, who catches it with ease.
- While still recording my teammates and I exchange high fives, and then at the end we all show good sportsmanship to the other team, shaking their hands as we pass by one

another.

- Then I hit the "save" button on the remote control. SA-WEET!

Tips for a Successful Exercise

- Use an old pair of glasses or sunglasses—you'll be taping them up, after all.
- Even though the lenses will be taped over, go ahead and close your eyes as you work through the exercise. You don't want any light distracting you from around the edges of the taped lenses.
- Try to feel the emotions as if the STINK episode were happening right now.
- Make sure you start your exercise in a quiet, semi-dark place.
- Re-write any STINK episode that made you feel angry, frustrated, guilty, ashamed, or scared.

The STINKIN' Summary

- No one is completely resistant to STINKIN' THINKIN'. Even the most positive people have to deal with STINKIN' THINKIN'.
- STINKIN' THINKIN' can cause you to do something you may regret for a very long time
- The key is to acknowledge the STINKIN' THINKIN' and change it to something SWEET.
- In team sports, always put your focus on the team's accomplishments and not your own. Do the same in the team that is your family and with any team of people with whom you work or play.

Thankfully, you can always record over any STINK episode you may have had in the past. Doing this exercise will help you know how you can handle STINKIN' thoughts in the future, and you'll have an easier time making a better choice the next time.

13
SWEET SCENTS
CREATE A SWEET GOAL

"Behave so the aroma of your actions may enhance the general sweetness of the atmosphere." —Henry David Thoreau (American Essayist, Poet, and Philosopher, 1817–1862)

STINKIN' THINKIN' Translation:
Practice good deeds daily to totally eliminate any bad ODORS you might have accumulated during any STINK mode, because good deeds fill the air with SA-WEET scents.

In The STINKIN' Squirt Story, STINKIN' THINKIN' led to a bunch of really bad choices—choices that hung around for a long time and took years to forgive. Does this mean that you're not allowed to make bad choices? Of course not! The main point is to become aware of STINKIN' THINKIN' and not to make decisions while you are experiencing a major STINK.

So, what happens if you have a SWEET thought about something you want to accomplish?

YOU CAN ACCOMPLISH SO MUCH WHEN YOU THINK OF A POSITIVE OUTCOME,

rather than a STINKIN' one. Nothing illustrates this better than the story below. When you keep your focus on the outcome you want, or reach for a goal, you can accomplish it. Sometimes it takes a while to achieve success, but

YOU WILL ACHIEVE IT IF YOU DON'T QUIT.

And just as surely, if you do quit, success won't be yours.

THE SA—WEET SOLAR SYSTEM SCIENCE FAIR SUCCESS

When I was twelve years old and in the seventh grade, I participated in my first science fair. As my science teacher read the rules and prizes for each of the categories, I had an idea. Whoever finished first in each category would be automatically entered into the district science fair. Now how cool would that be? I thought that if I put enough effort into it, I could actually win in the category I chose and go to the district fair. I didn't realize it at the time, but I was actually setting a goal for myself.

I decided to go out on a limb and create a science project on coffee. It was a very big current event topic at that time, so I thought it might carry some bonus points for me. I studied and researched coffee beans for weeks. I wrote and wrote, and then I wrote even more when I thought I should be done. I drew pictures of all the types of beans around the world, and I researched and wrote a lot about the coffee export business.

As I stared at my homemade poster board set-up, I suddenly thought, *You don't have a chance.* But then I did something that even surprised me: I changed my attitude and thought, *I think I can actually win a prize with this because of the awesome report I wrote for it.*

When all was said and done, the winners were announced while we were in our classroom. The announcer said, "And the social studies third place winner is... Billy King of the seventh grade." Now that was COOL! While I didn't win first place or get to go to the district fair, I *did* win a prize. I believe this only whetted my appetite to try even harder the next year.

In the eighth grade, I entered the science fair again and won second place. I have to admit that I was a bit disappointed with the results this time. So I had a choice. I could give up and not enter the next year's fair, or I could try even harder. I chose to try harder.

Our junior high school taught seventh, eighth, and ninth graders, so entering the fair in the ninth grade was my last shot at winning the first prize trophy I had set out to win two years earlier. This time I felt I needed to formulate an idea and plan my project on the very first day of the announcement of the fair. Instead of waiting weeks to start, I began working the very first week.

I have always been fascinated with space, and particularly with comets. So, I decided to do my project on them. This time I would use a wooden structure for a base instead of the flimsy cardboard I had used previously. I researched comets and studied them well into the night on many occasions.

I wanted to build something completely different, and I got the great idea of "recreating" a comet. I drilled holes into the wood frame and placed Christmas lights through them, simulating the orbit of a comet on one side of the board. I used cotton balls glued on to simulate the tail forming. I built our solar system on the opposite side using Styrofoam balls of different sizes. And because of all the hard work, I was rewarded with the greatest idea of all: a way to actually create a real-looking comet right there in the center of the board.

My idea was to put a box in the middle of the 3-panel board and paint a picture of the sun on it. Inside the box I mounted an old hair dryer. About four inches away from the hair dryer, I attached a turkey net bag with a chunk of dry ice in it. BINGO! Flip the switch and a comet was instantly born.

After all demonstrations were complete, the judging began. In the last period of the day, the winners were to be announced. As they went through all the different categories, they finally got to mine. "And the third place winner is…." It wasn't me, thank goodness. "And the second place winner is…." Not me again. I was nearly hyperventilating by this time. It was now down to the very last chance I had to accomplish my goal.

"And the first place winner is … Billy King for his project on comets." SCORE! I WON! I WON! I was actually jumping up in down in the air, and my classmates were all clapping for my accomplishment. Then the loud speaker clicked again. "Now we are going to award the overall science fair winners."

"And the overall third place winner is…." Not me. Darn! That would have been so cool to get an overall trophy. "And the runner-up winner is…" Not me. Okay, well, it was great winning first prize in my category, anyway. I turned and started talking to my fellow classmates when out of the blue the announcement came, "And the overall and Grand Prize goes to ... Billy King for his comet project. Congratulations, Billy, on a job well done. Billy will be representing our school along with all the first prize winners in next week's district fair."

I was completely speechless. The whole class was screaming in excitement. I felt like I was in a daze, and it was just a dream. *I won first place and the grand prize?* It almost didn't feel real that I had actually accomplished my goal *and won the grand prize too.*

I was escorted down the hall to claim my prizes and take a photo for the local newspaper. My grand prize trophy was about four feet tall and the buzz of excitement going on in my mind was overwhelming. I had done it! I had really done it!

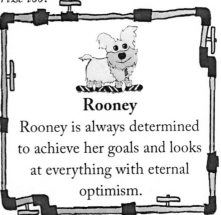

Rooney

Rooney is always determined to achieve her goals and looks at everything with eternal optimism.

I believe that I was rewarded with the incredible prizes because of my desire to win regardless of the odds, because I was able to visualize winning, and because I put my desire into action—all very positive attitudes and actions. I had a very clear goal. I accomplished that goal. I'd had a clear focus on what I wanted, I took action to study beyond what most others would do, and I followed my intuition as new ideas came to me along the process. I had no idea I could create a comet out of dry ice when I started. I started out thinking I could use lights to show the tail of the comet, and I wanted to impress the judges with a detailed report, since that had worked for me in the past. The dry ice idea didn't come until I was nearly finished with the project. But because I was in a positive zone, good ideas and energy flowed.

You can accomplish anything you desire. You just have to be clear about what you want and what you are willing to do to accomplish it. And you have to remain positive throughout the process and manifest that positivity in your actions. To help you get clear on just that, try the SUPER COOL exercise below.

STINKIN' EXERCISE:
SCORING A SA—WEET GOAL!

This STINKIN' exercise was designed to get you maximum results in whatever you want to accomplish. The average person thinks about 15,000 thoughts a day. That's a lot of thoughts! Just imagine if most of them were SA-WEET in nature. The difference between a good day and a bad day can easily be as simple as having more positive thoughts than STINKIN' thoughts. You can do that right?

This exercise will get you well on your path to SWEETNESS. By doing it, you'll discover that positively focusing on what you want is easier than you thought. Your improved attitude will not only bring better, more positive things to your life, but it will also be fun!

You will need the following items to complete this exercise:

- 1 white poster board
- a set of colored markers
- a pen
- a piece of 8 ½" x 11" paper
- 6 pictures of a soccer, basketball, football, or hockey goal. Each picture should be about 3 to 4 inches squared. If you can't find a picture, you can draw, color, and cut them out.

Step 1: For Starters
On the center of the top of the poster board, write the following: "My VICTORIES!" Using a different colored marker for each range, on the top of left-hand side of the poster board, write: "0–3 Months" and un-derline it. In the middle of the left-hand side of the board, write: "4–6 Months" and underline it. Next, near the bottom of the left-hand side of

the board, write: "7–12 Months."

Step 2: Setting Up A SA-WEET Goal

Get out your piece of paper and write: "0–3 Months" at the top of the page. Next, write down everything you can possibly think of that you would want in your life in the next three months. This includes all kinds of things like: make the school sports team, increase my math grade by 5 points, make a new friend, have a better attitude toward my siblings, etc. Anything you want to accomplish in the near future can be written down. I suggest that that you write down as many things as possible, at least ten things.

Immediately after the last item on the "0–3 Months" list, write "4–6 Months" and repeat writing down things you would like to happen in the next 4–6 months under that headline. Include items that relate to you personally, to your school, to your family, and to your friends. Some ideas might be to make the honor roll, to improve your batting average by 15 points, to get excited about something you love to do, to find a new hobby you'll love, etc. For this one, write as many things as you would like to have, would like to accomplish, or would like to happen to you. Some of the items could be repeated from the 0-3 month list.

Now turn the paper over and write: "7–12 Months" at the top. Follow the same guidelines as on the previous two lists. These will be longer-range goals, things that may take longer to accomplish. List as many things as you can, but this list may be smaller than the previous two. That is completely oaky. Things like being kinder to everyone, ending the school year on a high note, making several new totally awesome friends, placing in a band or choir competition, becoming a starter on your team, doing something kind every day for seven days, etc. This list will typically include things that will require more time and/or effort to accomplish.

Step 3: Getting Clarity

Get out your poster board and your list from Step 2. Pick two items from each list that you'd most like to accomplish or have happen. Only choose two of them and not any more than that. This will give you six items total, and make sure there are no repeats among these six. Once you have picked the items you want to include on the board, write them down using the same color as the heading they're under.

Next, identify one thing you could do that would help you to achieve each item on the poster board and then write that down to the right of the listed item. This is your action item. Repeat for each of the items on your list.

Here's an example: If you chose to increase your English grade by 5 points, an action item might be to find a friend who is a little older than you are or who has excellent grades in English to tutor you once a week. If you chose to increase your batting average by 15 points, an action item might be to hit off the batting tee or take extra hitting practice in the batting cages three times a week.

Step 4: Scheduling Practice

We all know that even great teams have to practice, and that goes for this exercise. First, schedule practice times, or times to focus solely on working toward your goal. Practice times should be no longer than 20 to 30 minutes, three times a week. Here is what a practice schedule might look like: Monday and Wednesday from 7:00–7:30 PM, Saturday 10:00–10:30 AM.

Step 5: The Game Plan

When it's time to practice, pull out your poster board. Read through the entire list, including the action items. Think about them for a bit and pick just one action to do and then do it. Each practice period should be spent doing one and only one item on your list.

Remember that practice does not make perfect. Perfect practice makes perfect! This means that you must make sure not to miss any practices—and that you must take the practice time seriously.

Step 6: Scoring a Goal

Once you have achieved an item on your list, you have scored a GOAL! Now you get to take one of the six pictures of the soccer, basketball, football, or hockey goal and glue it over the appropriate section of your poster.

Then you have to say out loud and with enthusiasm the following: "**He shoots... He SCOOOOOOOOOOOOOOOORRRRRRES!**" or "**She shoots... She SCOOOOOOOOOOOOOOOOOOORRRRRRRRRR RRES!**" As you do this, make a fist with each hand, raise those fists in the air, and then end by saying, "**YESSSSSSSS! Who's the *MAN*? I AM! I ROCK!**" Feel free to add your own awesome affirmations too!

Repeat step 6 each time one of your goals is accomplished.

Tips for a Successful Exercise

- Take your time when deciding what you want to do during the time frames.
- When you first start, start small and stick to the game plan.
- If you don't feel you are accomplishing what you want fast enough, schedule one more practice period per week or extend the current ones by 10 or 15 minutes.
- Share your successes with your family and friends. Get them involved in what you want to achieve. They will often provide an "assist" to your goal.
- Make your poster board as colorful as it can be. Decorate it to the max!
- Place your board where you will see it every day.
- When you see colors that match up to the color you chose on the board, take just a moment to visualize yourself achieving that goal.

The STINKIN' Summary

- Everyone makes choices each day, and they can be good ones or bad ones.
- Never make choices when you are in STINK mode.
- If you make a bad choice, don't dwell on it. Decide right now to make a different choice next time.
- Setting goals can be fun.
- Scoring goals is even better!
- Allow others to "assist" you in scoring your goals.

When you make choices while in STINK mode, you can be sure that the choices you make will not be in your best interest. However, when you visualize what you want to happen, you can be sure that you're one SWEET SMELLIN' puppy! One way to accomplish what you want to happen is to create goals. And achieving goals can be really fun when you do the exercise in this chapter.

14
THE STINKIN' CONCLUSION
TYING ALL THE STINK TOGETHER

"Know yourself. Don't accept your dog's admiration as conclusive evidence that you are wonderful." —Ann Landers (Advice columnist, 1918-2002)

STINKIN' THINKIN' Translation:

Be honest with yourself about how you act. And then get
rid of STINKIN' THINKIN' because you will want
to be friends with more than just your pet.

By now you are aware that negative thoughts STINK! This is a serious STINKIN' matter. STINKIN' THINKIN' is nothing but having and continuing to have negative thinking. This negative thinking can bring a bunch of STINKIN' things into your life when you're not aware of it. As you work through the exercises in this book, you will slowly start to become aware of your STENCH and things you never thought about before. It will bring out a bunch of STINKIN' stuff that has been crammed into your head for a long time. The purpose of this book is to open your mind and let out some of that built-up garbage. When you start to become conscious of all the wonderful things there are in your life, you're certain to begin to experience more of it. And who wouldn't want more of that?

Everyone is a magnet. What? Yes, everyone is a magnet. You are either a magnet for happiness, joy, peace, love, excitement, and success, or you are a magnet for STINKIN' things like anger, frustration, worry, and fear. Yikes! The choice is yours and only yours to make.

People either have a positive influence on others or a negative one. A great goal is to strive to be someone who lives in happiness and joy. When you achieve this, your happiness and joy become as contagious as any STINKIN' THINKIN'. You can then have a positive influence on other STINKIN' people. This is a great feat because as you help other STINKIN' people, other people will also want to help you. It's a great cycle to start spinning in your life!

When you clear out your STINKIN' trash, you'll start to attract new SA-WEET friends and relationships. At the very minimum, you'll be a positive example for any of your STINKIN' friends and offer them a different way to look at things. Sometimes just by having a positive attitude, you can shift the STENCH right out of others. You STINK shifter, you!

IF *YOU* CLEAR OUT THE STINK FROM WHAT *YOU* THINK, WHAT *YOU* SAY, AND WHAT *YOU* DO; *YOU* WILL DRASTICALLY IMPACT IN A POSITIVE WAY WHAT *YOU* SEE, TOUCH, HEAR, TASTE, AND SMELL. *YES!* ISN'T THAT SWEET?

There are some major limiting factors that keep you from living a STINK-FREE life. They start and end with your emotions. When you're happy or excited, it's like you're emitting a tune like "Don't Worry, Be Happy." You virtually give off a positive glow. Nothing bothers you, and when something negative comes up, you look for an opportunity to change it or to use it as a learning experience.

Stanky
Stanky will remain a nuisance to others until he becomes aware of STINKIN' THINKIN' and works to change it.

When you're in an emotional STINKIN' state of anger, worry, doubt, and fear; it's like you're singing off-key or giving off a dim, dull, foggy light. Oh no, friend! Don't go there!

Now comes the SWEET part. As you work through the exercises, positive things will start to happen to you. At first, you might think that they're just coincidences, but think again. Each positive event leads to other positive events, and before you know it you're like the indestructible "Iron Man," soaring through the air, eliminating STINK all over the place. You'll be a STINK crop duster eliminating ODOR with swift sweeps of SWEET SMELLS for everyone to enjoy. Yeah, you'll be that good!

Negative thoughts STINK, but you sure don't anymore! You have:

- become aware of your thoughts
- found ways to eliminate negative thinking
- done exercises to help you focus on positive thinking
- developed techniques for dealing with negative people and even helping them to embrace a more positive attitude

And in embracing positivity, you are SA-WEET and ready to enjoy every benefit a positive attitude brings! Enjoy every single minute of each day, and as you encounter STINKIN' people in your STINK-FREE life, share some of what you know. It just might leave them SA-WEET, too!

BONUS: Turn Your STINKIN' Life Into Greatness

Enjoy the free bonuses and all the fun stuff at www.idontstink.com.

BONUS MATERIAL!
WHICH STINKER ARE YOU LIKE?

Take the quiz below and find out.
Are you SA-WEET or just another STINKER!

Answer each question below how YOU would best answer it.

1.   Now that I have read this STINKIN' book, I _____.
   a.   Didn't learn a STINKIN' thing about nothin'.
   b.   Realize that there are a bunch of STINKIN' people around me.
   c.   Value becoming aware of my STINKIN' THINKIN'.
   d.   Recognize that I have choices. Some are good while some just STINK.
   e.   Understand that I am responsible for my own STINKIN' and SA-WEET thoughts.

2.   When I am in a STINK mode, I can use visualization to _____.
   a.   Picture how stupid this STINKIN' book really is.
   b.   See other people getting a lot out of this STINKIN' book.
   c.   Change my thought process, but certainly not during a STINK mode.
   d.   Change my thought process.
   e.   Picture myself in my mind's eye experiencing exactly what I want.

3.   STINKIN' THINKIN' serves a purpose. And that purpose is to
_____.

    a. Prove to everyone how much I STINK.

    b. Inform me that there are others around me that really STINK.

    c. Discover that I am in a STINK mode and should do something about it.

    d. Decide whether to change my thoughts and smell SWEET, or continue to STINK.

    e. Let me know that I am experiencing something I do not STINKIN' want.

4.   In the terms of STINKIN' THINKIN', the phrase "like attracts like" means _____.

    a. I have no STINKIN' idea what you are asking.

    b. Other people STINK because that is what they want.

    c. You attract STINKIN' people that you are most like.

    d. I attract people that I am most like and they may STINK or be SA-WEET.

    e. I am responsible for attracting the kinds of people I want in my life.

5.   Wayne Dyer's quote, "If you change the way you look at things, the things you look at change." means _____?

    a. Absolutely nothing to me. I can't change the way things are by simply changing how I STINKIN' look at them.

    b. People with a bad case of the STINK eye need to change how they look at things.

    c. If I stare at something long enough, they might not STINK so badly.

    d. When you look for the good, you see the good. When you look for the bad, you see that too.

    e. When I look for the beauty in all things, I see more beauty in them naturally.

6.   Why is STINK breath one of the most contagious forms of STINKIN' THINKIN'?

  a. What? My STINK breath has nothing to do with STINKIN' THINKIN' so stop asking me so many stupid STINKIN' questions.

  b. It's only contagious if you are around STINKIN' people.

  c. STINK breath could be cured if everyone would just keep their STINKIN' mouths shut.

  d. Because if one person says something that really STINKS, others typically join in and say a bunch of STINKIN' things themselves.

  e. It's contagious because when I say something that STINKS, others will join in on the STINKIN' conversation.

7.   One of the best ways to get STINKIN' THINKIN' out of your head is to _____?

  a. Tell everyone about my STINKIN' THINKIN' so I don't have to STINKIN' deal with it.

  b. Keep it to myself so no one knows that I am one STINKIN' dude (or dudette).

  c. Understand what I'm thinking about, tell all my STINKIN' friends about it, and complain to them about it.

  d. Take out my STINKIN' trash and dump it in the closest land fill.

  e. Take out my STINKIN' trash daily so I become aware of my STINKIN' THINKIN'.

My Score is _____

How to score the Quiz

For each answer, give the point total from below and add up the total score:

> All "a" answers = 2 points
> All "b" answers = 4 points
> All "c" answers = 6 points
> All "d" answers = 8 points
> All "e" answers = 10 points

Once you have added up your scores, go to www.idontstink.com/bonus-quiz to see which character you are most like.

THE CHARACTERS

Mary Elizabeth Smith
AKA "Sweetie"

Winthrop Ferguson Alexander III
AKA "Stanky"

Rena Rae Robinson
AKA "Rosie"

Larry Lenard Landry
AKA "Lavy"

Fleuretta Danielle De Lorme
AKA "Sugar"

Billy Joe Bob
AKA "Rotten"

Hans Vieden
AKA "Bruiser"

Sammy Sherman Sanders
AKA "Skids"

Tabitha Tessa Tomlinson
AKA "Twiggy"

Roonicans Reina Reynard
AKA "Rooney"

The **STINK TANK Newsletter** – Sign up for a TOTALLY free newsletter designed for kids. It includes regular sections like:

> **The STINK of the Month** – A recent news article that contains something that STINKS.

> **STINKIN' Cool Dudes** – Interviews, articles a contributions from some super cool people.

> **SMELLIN' Salts** – Exercises to help you get the TINK out.

> **SWEET Scents** – A positive news article that may may not have anything to do with smells.

> **SA-WEET Sayings** – Inspirational quotes to help focus on the positive.

> **STINKISMS** – Positive quotes with a TWIST.

> **Kind Deeds Indeed** – Ideas, suggestions and chall for you to do kind deeds.

To sign up for the FA-REE newsletter, go to www.idontstink.com, select the "Free Stuff" barrel on the left hand side of the page.

Daily Positive Points – Emails sent to your inbox every morning, Monday through Friday. Each one contains a message plus an inspirational quote. There are also videos on Friday and much more.

To sign up for the FA-FREE daily emails, go to www.idontstink.com, then select the "Free Stuff" barrel on the left hand side of the page.

ABOUT THE AUTHOR

Bill King is a writer, speaker, certified trainer and mentor. A master of designing and implementing processes to simplify complex issues with amazing results, he used this gift to design fun, exciting and educational ideas to help kids deal with negativity, low self-esteem, bullying and anger. He teaches kids positive thinking, kindness, forgiveness and awareness in a way they can relate to.

His website www.idontstink.com teaches kids from a completely different point of view. The premise is negative thoughts stink. Using humor to break down the barriers many people have, Bill provides an entertaining atmosphere that promotes learning that will stick. Check out the STINK-o-city quiz to see how badly you STINK! Benefit from tons of easy-to-follow exercises, and enter your kind deeds into the kindness meter. Issue kindness challenges and be challenged yourself—all because you want to SMELL sa-weet!

CPSIA information can be obtained at www.ICGtesting.com
Printed in the USA
BVOW02s0120260216

437899BV00002B/97/P